A Time to Wait

A Time to Wait

Bible insights on trusting God's timing

Liz Morris

Text copyright © Liz Morris 2001

The author asserts the moral right
to be identified as the author of this work

Published by
BRF
First floor, Elsfield Hall
15–17 Elsfield Way, Oxford OX2 8EP
ISBN 1 84101 048 0

First published 2001
10 9 8 7 6 5 4 3 2 1 0

All rights reserved

Acknowledgments
Unless otherwise stated, scripture quotations are taken from the
Holy Bible, New International Version, copyright © 1973, 1978,
1984 by International Bible Society, and are used by permission of
Hodder & Stoughton Limited. All rights reserved. 'NIV' is a
registered trademark of International Bible Society. UK trademark
number 1448790.

Scripture quotations from the Revised Standard Version of the Bible
(RSV) are copyright © 1946, 1952, 1971 by the Division of
Christian Education of the National Council of the Churches of
Christ in the United States of America, and are used by permission.
All rights reserved.

The Holy Bible, Living Bible Edition (LB), copyright © Tyndale
House Publishers 1971.

Extract from 'Thorns in the Straw' by Graham Kendrick. Copyright
© 1994 Make Way Music, PO Box 263, Croydon, Surrey, CR9 5AP,
UK. International copyright secured. All rights reserved. Used by
permission.

A catalogue record for this book is available from the British Library

Printed and bound in Great Britain by Omnia Books Limited,
Glasgow

Contents

Foreword

Now Jesus loved Martha and her sister and Lazarus. Yet when he heard that Lazarus was sick, he stayed where he was two more days.
JOHN 11:5–6

If only God didn't love us so much! How can we read those verses from John's Gospel without, in our hearts, screaming a protest at Jesus' refusal to comply with their plea to come at once? We all hate waiting, seeing it as a complete waste of time and harbouring suspicions of indifference on God's part. Yet learning to wait is part of the process of growing to maturity, as Rudyard Kipling suggests in his poem, 'If'. 'If you can wait and not grow tired of waiting… You'll be a man, my son.'

God is so determined to mature us that he will at times be silent or still when we want him to speak or act. He in turn is waiting for us to grow—in grace, in prayer, in love, in trusting him even when, as with Job, all the powers of hell are allowed to attack and oppose us. I say again, if only God didn't love us so much!

For some years now I have watched Liz and David Lyle Morris lay hold of God in good times and bad. The contents of this book have been drawn from their experiences as well as from their study of the word of God. We are indebted to Liz for sharing her insights with such wisdom and love.

Faith Forster

Introduction:
Instant Generation

Nowadays we live in a world of fast cars, fast food and instant credit. We expect to phone a helpline to arrange a mortgage in about 20 minutes and get cash whenever we feel like it from 'holes in the wall'. Instead of a leisurely afternoon tea served to our table in a café we queue for a burger and milkshake. The Internet gives us immediate communication through e-mail. We can have a conversation via a screen with someone on the other side of the world, as if they were in the room with us. On cable TV we can shop in an instant, while some supermarkets let us scan our shopping as we go, using the computer labels on the groceries. Why wait in line if we don't have to? And if *we* are the instant generation, the mind boggles to think at what speed our children will expect things to happen.

It hasn't always been like this. We do not have to look hundreds of years into the past to see how standards and expectations have changed. Even in the 1950s life was very different. Britain was more like pre-1989 Eastern Europe with rationing still commonplace and queuing practically an art form! On Fridays, the weekly pay day for most manual workers, women would line up outside the butcher's shop to buy the meat for the weekend. Most people did not have cars, so they walked, cycled or went by train or bus, which usually meant standing for some time at a railway station or bus stop (maybe some things have not changed so much!). Those were the days when it took six weeks to sail to New Zealand, rather than the 24 hours that an aeroplane flight takes now. Before the days of washing machines, laundering the family clothes was a major household chore which took hours. Just 30 years ago, I remember my mother having to put our clothes through a mangle before hanging them out to dry. Most homes had no television and the computer game had not even been invented, so there was more emphasis on spending leisure time as an extended family with singsongs, parties and board games.

Relationships were conducted differently too. Engagements as long as two to five years were acceptable because couples did not marry until they had enough money to set up a nice home—or at least the best they could afford. Sex before marriage was rarely an option; in pre-pill days, most people waited until the wedding night.

Like society in general, the church-going population has experienced major changes too. Overall church attendance has declined, especially among young people, but there has also been a growth of the 'New Church' movement. These churches meet in schools and community centres and have moved away from the more traditional type of service. When I was a teenager attending a relatively 'middle of the road' Church of Scotland congregation, it was not unusual for the youth group to sit through a morning service which included a 40-minute sermon. The minister did not feel it necessary to jazz up the service with drama or introduce gimmicks like coloured slide shows to hold our attention. When the youth group led a service, we felt we were being radical if we used choruses instead of hymns. I remember an elderly lady in our church giving her testimony and telling us how she had spent ten years praying and waiting for a particular event to happen. To a teenager then, it seemed for ever. Even now as an adult, I view with awe anybody who could wait that long for something.

Many congregations these days expect services to be

short, sharp and to the point. We want sketches, video clips, interviews, and the latest worship songs rather than hymns. The preacher tends to be discouraged from talking for more than ten minutes because people grow restless. Sometimes it feels as if our services, like our society, have grown too geared to an instant culture. Of course most people would agree that, to some extent, we need to reflect our society. We want church to be 'relevant', but where has the quest for a 'relevant' church taken us? Sometimes I attend a reflective service where I may be asked to pray longer than in a 'normal' service, or spend time meditating on God's word. To be honest, I find it tough going. Sitting still and quietly reflecting on God is something that many of us struggle with these days. More and more, it seems that we have lost the ability to wait and listen to God. We are happy if God gives us a 'Yes' answer to our prayers and we can even cope if he says 'No', but if he says 'wait' we want to know how long— a week, a month, maybe two months? Surely not years.

I visited the Toronto Christian Fellowship (formerly the Airport Vineyard Church), about three years after it first hit the headlines for the dramatic way in which people experienced God in the services. I had heard some strange stories about what went on at the church, involving people making weird noises and falling over 'in the Spirit'. I was more than a little apprehensive about visiting, however. I had a sense that God wanted me to go, and be open to hearing what he might reveal to me about my future. When I arrived at the church I found there were no song books— instead a computer projected all the words of the songs on to a large screen. By the end of the service a recording of the preacher's talk was already available so that overseas visitors could take it back home—the speed of it all was impressive! By the end of the first meeting, it was obvious that the rumours I had heard were exaggerated. The leaders came over as very humble people and the main impression I got was that they wanted to serve God to the best of their abilities. God's presence at their meetings was clearly demonstrated in the peaceful atmosphere and the joy in the people's faces.

I went to Toronto anticipating that I would in some way hear from God. I hoped that either through a Bible reading, through the speaker or even through the person sitting next to me, God would somehow show me what he wanted for my life. Although my expectations were high, God had a few surprises for me. It was not until the last night that I felt God speak to me and when he did speak, through the message that night, he was saying, 'Wait'. To say that my initial reaction was one of disappointment would be an understatement. After travelling halfway around the world, leaving at home my husband and baby son (both of whom I was missing dreadfully), I was expecting something startling and instantly life-changing. Not just 'wait'.

When I came home, I immediately decided to look in the Bible to see if I could find anybody else who, like me, had felt God tell them to wait. I wanted to see how they coped with the time of waiting because I urgently needed some help to do so. What I found amazed me: in having to wait I was in very good company. Many of the biblical characters whom I most respected had to endure long periods of waiting for God to fulfil his promises to them. Not only did they have to wait a long time for God, but some of them were not at all patient. I realized that in developing the necessary patience for waiting, I would have to unlearn the way I thought, and that I had been influenced, not just by society but by some of the church teachings too. As it was, I expected instant solutions and answers to all my problems, just like most of my friends.

Maybe you feel you received a promise from God a while

ago and that you are still waiting for something to happen? Maybe you have seen this promise fulfilled in part, but along the way have made mistakes and now you fear that God will not deliver on the rest of the promise? If so, then I hope you will find this book helpful. I have chosen well-known biblical characters and I study the events which show how they had to learn to wait for God's timing—and how they, and the people around them, responded to that challenge. Some of them saw only a partial fulfilment of God's promise to them, some never saw their promise fulfilled at all during their life-time, while others saw it completed. Maybe you will find help in your present situation by relating to one of the Bible characters who has gone through a similar 'waiting game' to you. Maybe you will learn something from their mistakes and successes. Above all, I hope that you will be encouraged in your time of waiting and be open to learning the lessons God may have in store for you.

But they who wait for the Lord shall renew their strength, they shall mount up with wings like eagles, they shall run and not be weary, they shall walk and not faint.

ISAIAH 40:31 (RSV)

1

Abraham and Sarah:
The 25-Year Labour

'I am God Almighty; walk before me, and be blameless. And I will make my covenant between me and you, and will multiply you exceedingly.'
GENESIS 17:1–2 (RSV)

Abraham and Sarah came from a society that worshipped idols and statues of many different gods. When they left home in obedience to God's call, their relationship grew with the one true God. They learnt to accept waiting as a normal part of life, even though at times it put them under great strain. Even though they often made mistakes, God continued to bless them. They learnt that he could right their wrongs, and that obedience to him, the living and loving God, was more important than anything else.

First encounter with God

Abram, as he is first known, is 75 years old when God begins to speak to him. Abram's immediate response is astonishing—he immediately does what God says! In the city of Ur where Abram lived, people worshipped many gods, and the idea of a personal, direct encounter with one God would have been extraordinary. Leaving your home, uprooting your family and following direct instructions from this one God would have been viewed as more than a little mad, especially as Abram did not even know where he was going. In response to criticism he would have said, 'I am leaving because the one and only God has told me to, though I do not know exactly where I am going. But he did tell me that he would guide me.' Abram had an amazing degree of faith and he must have had such a powerful experience of God that it seemed worth giving up everything for.

Over the years Abram and his wife Sarai (later Sarah) received a number of promises from God. Genesis 12:1–3, tells us the first promise: 'Leave your own country behind you, and your own people, and go to the land I will guide you to. If you do, I will cause you to become the father of a great nation; I will bless you and make your name famous, and you will be a blessing to many others. I will bless those who bless you and curse those who curse you; and the entire world will be blessed because of you' (LB).

This promise must have both encouraged and frightened Abram. God promised him land—something tangible that Abram would be able to see realized or not—but the main promise was that Abram would be the father of a great nation, even though Sarai could not have children. And if we look more closely at this first encounter with God, we see that Abram is asked to do something extremely difficult—to leave everything. Only if he does this will God give him the promised blessings. We are told that Abram was a wealthy man: he must have enjoyed a comfortable life. Leaving everything he knew for the unknown was a great risk, but Abram did it. And Sarai went with him. Either Abram had convinced her that this God he was following was worth it— or maybe she was just trusting in her husband.

Abram did not, however, follow God's word to the letter because he took his nephew Lot along. We discover later that Lot caused Abram much trouble. Maybe God knew what he was doing when he suggested leaving the relatives behind?

This part of Abram's life amazes me. If God had spoken to me when I was not a Christian and told me to leave everything and head for an unknown destination, I would not have listened to the rest of what God had to say! I would have assumed that I had imagined the voice of God, and I would have certainly refused to involve my family in such an uncertain situation. Or I would have decided that God's message was for someone else. This is in stark contrast to Abram's reaction. We can learn from him to be more spontaneous, more open to God's guidance. What we should remember is that God knows our circumstances before he asks something of us. We may be stronger and better equipped than we know for the task ahead.

A special relationship

Perhaps the most exciting aspect of this part of the story is how God honoured Abram as though he were an old friend. We would only make a special promise to a friend if we had known them for years, but in God's very first encounter with Abram, he offers him more than he could ever have dreamed. And in return he asks for obedience. God does not wait to make us promises until we have been Christians for a certain number of years—checking us out, as it were. All too often we feel as if we have to pass some kind of spiritual assault course before he will speak to us. Looking at Abram's life, this appears not to be true.

God also honours Abram by saying that whoever he blesses or curses, God will bless or curse (Genesis 12:3). He is already indicating to Abram how special this new relationship will be, making significant even the words Abram speaks.

So Abram leaves his familiar surroundings and starts travelling. When they arrive in Canaan (Genesis 12:5), God promises that he will give this land to Abram's descendants (the promised great nation). But after building an altar and worshipping God, Abram goes on to Egypt, not because God told him to, but because of famine in the land. Rather than consulting with God he relies on his common sense, going in search of food. As the story goes on to tell, this gets him into serious trouble.

Even though Abram had just had another intimate encounter with God, with a further revelation of the promise, he forgot to wait patiently for the next step. Instead he reacted to the very next circumstance by taking hasty action without recourse to God. Maybe you recognize yourself in Abram at this point? We can be walking steadily in the will of God; then an opportunity arises—promotion at work, for example—and we do not consult God before accepting it. We assume it must be right and it may only be much later that we realize it was not necessarily best for us—it was not God's intention.

Times of testing

When Abram and Sarai arrive in Egypt, they decide not to admit to Sarai being Abram's wife, to protect themselves or, more particularly, Abram, who fears he will be killed if another man wants to take the beautiful Sarai as his wife (Genesis 12:12). And when Pharaoh hears of Sarai's beauty he invites her to join his household, giving Abram many gifts as payment for her (Genesis 12:16). At this point, Abram may have given up on Sarai as lost, no longer part of God's promises to him. Once a woman became part of the Pharaoh's harem, it was unlikely that she would walk free again. It is God, then, who has to intervene to save Sarai. A plague comes upon the household, and Pharaoh is shocked to find out that Sarai is Abram's wife. He returns her to her husband and has them both escorted out of Egypt (Genesis 12:20).

God knew that Sarai was part of his promise to Abram, even though Abram himself doubted that in Egypt. We now see Abram returning to Canaan and his altar once again to worship God (Genesis 13:3–4), returning to the old intimacy. Despite a major error of judgment, he has enough faith to trust that God will accept him back and so he goes back to the place where he last heard directly from God. When we feel that we have grown far away from God, perhaps through making a mistake, it can help to visit a place or a person through whom we heard from God in the past. It reminds us of the times when we felt close to God, when we heard him speaking clearly and unmistakably. If we are enduring a time of waiting, we can feel as if God has given up on us, but in looking back we remember what God has done for us in the past.

Abram's experiences, in Egypt and later, also remind us that after times of remarkable spiritual encounters with God, times of great testing, waiting or long silences may follow. Naturally we may feel deflated when the time of the special encounter passes, and when the next time of testing comes along we assume that God has let us down, that the closeness of the special encounter meant nothing. In fact, God may be waiting for us to develop and mature, so that he can work further in our lives.

Promises repeated

Over the next year, God reinforces his original promises to Abram. Again he promises land as far as the eye can see and descendants as the dust of the earth (Genesis 13:14–16). We then get a small insight into the growing relationship between Abram and his God, because this time Abram begins to question how the promises can be fulfilled —especially the promise of descendants, because Sarai is infertile and he still has no son, no natural heir.

Like Abram, we too can question God about his plans for our lives. Looking elsewhere in the Bible, we find Moses, who questions God at the burning bush (Exodus 3), Mary the mother of Jesus, who questions the angel about how she will conceive when she is not married (Luke 1:34), and Gideon, who tests God by laying out fleeces (Judges 6:36–40). Like them, we find that if we ask God for help, for answers, before acting in obedience to his command he is gracious and answers in some way, even when we have put conditions on our response.

Surrogate child

After the events in Egypt, we have a ten-year gap in the narrative. No events are recorded and life probably just went on as normal. God was waiting for the right time to enact the next part of his promise. The temptation would be strong to think that God was being inactive. Perhaps he needed a helping hand?

Trying to help God out can complicate not only your own situation but that of others too! We do not know whether Sarai just got fed up with waiting or whether she decided to solve the problem of an heir in the customary fashion. Maybe she felt she should do something because it was her failure to have children that was preventing God from fulfilling his promise. So Sarai offered her handmaiden Hagar to Abram (Genesis 16:1–3). Hagar's son would become Abram's legitimate heir, thus fulfilling God's promise to them. But there was one major problem with this arrangement: she did not consult God first. And the mess that resulted needed God's intervention to remedy it.

Delighted with her fertility, Hagar taunts Sarai, Sarai blames Abram, Abram washes his hands of the whole situation, Sarai beats Hagar and Hagar runs away (Genesis

16:6). Sarai's attempt at a solution has made everyone unhappy. Hagar runs to the desert and encounters an angel who tells her to return to her mistress. She comes back to Sarai, having had her very own encounter with God, and then gives birth to Ishmael.

I feel particularly sorry for Sarai. She did what I would have done—she found a practical solution to a problem. She had decided quite sensibly that because she could not humanly have children, God would obviously fulfil the promise by the only other practical solution—surrogacy. But common sense can be a dangerous thing if it excludes the workings of a supernatural God.

Some close friends of ours, Grant and Emily, had spent four years trying to conceive a baby. Someone in their church believed God had specifically told them that Emily would be pregnant by the time she was 26 years old. The couple had numerous tests and hormone treatment without any sign of success. They were due for more serious medical intervention but then, a week before her 26th birthday, Emily found out she was pregnant. What a time of joy! The amazing thing about this couple is that throughout that time of waiting to conceive, they did not grow bitter. They willingly looked after other people's children, and had become an adopted aunt and uncle to our own young son. They held fast to the promise that they felt God had given them, despite the discouraging prognosis.

When everything seems to conspire against the promise we believe God has made to us, we can do nothing else except hold on to the word of God.

A change of name

Returning to the adventures of Abram and Sarai, we find that Abram had not heard from God for 13 years after the birth of Ishmael (Genesis 17:1–2). Presumably during that time Abram treated Ishmael as nothing less than his first-born, his rightful heir and the realization of God's promise to him. He is 99 years old when God speaks to him again (Genesis 17:1–5) and makes a covenant, an eternal and unbreakable promise, with Abram. He promises that Abram will be the father of not just one but many nations and then changes Abram's name to Abraham, meaning 'father of many'. And this time God declares that the contract he is making with Abraham will stand from generation to generation and that his descendants will inherit the land of Canaan. And this is a two-way promise: in return God requires Abraham to circumcise all the males in his household, both family and servants (Genesis 17:9–14), as a sign that he and his descendants would keep their side of the promise.

God then changes Sarai's name to Sarah, meaning 'Princess'—an astonishing name to give an old woman, but indicating how God can look at the very heart of a person, not just their outward appearance. God then makes the amazing promise that Sarah will have a son and that she will be the mother of many nations (Genesis 17:15–16). When he hears this, Abraham actually laughs inwardly, and says in reply, 'Yes, do bless Ishmael' (Genesis17:18, LB). So God repeats himself and promises the birth of another son, from Sarah, by the following year. Abraham had assumed that God was talking about Ishmael—it is as if he just was not listening to what God was saying. So God graciously repeats himself.

Abraham's faith shines through all his dealings with God. Although he debates and doubts, he ultimately obeys. The New Testament shows how we too can be like Abraham through faith: 'Understand, then, that those who believe are children of Abraham... So those who have faith are blessed along with Abraham, the man of faith' (Galatians 3:7, 9).

Silent laughter

God's next encounter is perhaps the most dramatic, the most physical, and is for Sarah's benefit as well, drawing her closer into the covenant relationship. Genesis 18:1–15 tells the episode in detail: three men visit Abraham's camp and he lays on a feast 'fit for a king' for them. As they are eating, the strangers ask after Sarah and dramatically repeat the promise that Abraham has already received—that by next year Sarah will have a son. Sarah is eavesdropping at the tent door, and her reaction is the same as Abraham's earlier: she laughs silently to herself! And then 'the Lord'—God— speaks and asks why Sarah is laughing. Does she doubt the power of God?

For the first time, Sarah has heard for herself a promise from God which directly concerns her, but despite her experience of God's power at work (for example, God rescuing her in Egypt and sending his angel to save Hagar), she still cannot believe that this promise could really come true. Yet God has decided that the time has come for Isaac to be born: as we hear again in the New Testament, 'By faith Abraham, even though he was past age—and Sarah herself was barren—was enabled to become a father because he considered him faithful who had made the promise' (Hebrews 11:11).

Sometimes our own view of the past can cloud our vision for the future and our ability to trust God. Looking back, though, can show us how God has previously answered us, perhaps in ways we did not expect. And looking back can help us to see that our expectations are often much lower than they could be. What is impossible to us is fully possible to God—and his timing is always perfect. He often brings us to the point where we have tried every alternative before realizing that we can do nothing, that we must be totally reliant on him. Then he can act in power.

Now that God has promised a son to Abraham and Sarah, more surely than ever, we might expect that from now on Abraham will trust God fully in every part of his life. In fact, what happens next is a repeat of the episode in Egypt. Abraham moves south for a while, telling the people there that Sarah is his sister (Genesis 20:1–2). The king in that region decides to take Sarah to his palace. God intervenes and tells the king in a dream that he is as good as dead because he has taken a married women. It is only through the prayers of Abraham that the king and his household are saved, the women having lost their own fertility as a punishment for what has been done to Sarah (Genesis 20:6–18).

In a strange way, this sorry story is a comfort to us. It shows that even if we make the same mistake twice—even a serious mistake—God will still forgive us. God forgave Abraham for his weakness, even though it came after such a powerful encounter with God's living presence.

The promised son

Abraham and Sarah had waited 25 years for God to fulfil his promise. They had been through many difficulties and made numerous mistakes, but at last the promised son arrived. We can only imagine what Abraham and, especially, Sarah were feeling on the day that Isaac was born. They had seen their hearts' desire made real. I remember how I felt when our son was born. I thought he was a miracle and I had not waited 25 years!

How simple it would be if the story of Abraham finished there with a neat happy ending, Abraham and Sarah had their long-awaited son, Isaac. For eight years we can suppose they led a normal family life. Then God intervenes once again and gives Abraham a horrific command: he must offer Isaac to him as a sacrifice. Abraham may well have been familiar with child sacrifice, as a number of ancient religions required it from their followers, but he must have been appalled that God was asking him to do this. God challenges Abraham's faith in him to the uttermost, asking him to lay down the most precious gift in his life, the son for whom he had waited so long. The whole promised future, the whole covenant made with God, looks as if it will be destroyed.

For three days Abraham travels with Isaac, carrying the weight of the knowledge of what God is asking of him. He builds an altar, lays Isaac on it and raises a knife to kill him. Only then does an angel intervene to save Isaac. Abraham feared God enough not to withhold his son, yet had faith enough to believe God's promise that his descendants would come through Isaac.

According to Proverbs 1:7–8, 'The fear of the Lord is the beginning of knowledge, but fools despise wisdom and discipline.' It is almost impossible for us nowadays to understand the right fear of God that made Abraham willing to sacrifice his own son. Another word for this 'right fear' is 'awe', meaning 'wonder or admiration charged with reverence'. Abraham did not obey God because he was afraid but because he was in awe of God.

Today the concept of personal rights is very important to most people. We may even expect everything to be fair in our relationship with God. Some of us have been brought up with so little respect for authority that we do not understand the concept of a healthy fear or respect of God. We may think that being a Christian is only about love, and that fearing God is an unhealthy Old Testament belief. Abraham's willingness to sacrifice Isaac was an exceptional test of his reverence for God, and it is unlikely that we will have to face something of similar magnitude. We will certainly be tested, though, and we should ask ourselves whether we can let our faith and trust in God grow as strong as Abraham's.

We may be tempted to look at somebody like Abraham and doubt whether we could ever be as strong in faith as he was. Abraham became a remarkable man of faith over many years. He made many mistakes along the way, but he always humbly returned to restore his relationship with the God he both feared and trusted. We too can build a faith like Abraham's if we are willing to learn from our mistakes and nurture a relationship with God which is as honest as Abraham's.

Like Abraham, we should long to become God's friend and for us this has been made possible by the death and resurrection of Jesus Christ. 'For this reason Christ is the mediator of a new covenant, that those who are called may receive the promised eternal inheritance' (Hebrews 9:15). We no longer have to live under the restrictions of the old covenant, but can have an intimate relationship with God because of the sacrifice of his Son and the new kingdom revealed by this.

Abraham and Sarah did not always wait patiently for God to work. They tried to solve things for themselves, they lied, they doubted; yet God was faithful to the promises he had made. We too can know this patient, loving God, and if we stay in a close relationship with him, his hand will direct our lives, mistakes and all.

'Abraham believed God and it was reckoned to him as righteousness'; and he was called the friend of God.
JAMES 2:23 (RSV)

2

Joseph: From Pit to Prince

Joseph's master took him and put him in prison, the place where the king's prisoners were confined.
GENESIS 39:20

Joseph is a young man whose circumstances seem, on the face of it, to conspire against God ever being able to fulfil the promises given to him. He actually spent 22 years, some of them in prison, waiting for those promises to come true —maturing into the person God intended him to become by enduring all kinds of difficult and challenging circumstances. And as we will see, in God's plans, circumstances can be turned to good, even if they were originally intended for evil.

Shepherd boy

At the start of the story, Joseph is the eleventh of twelve sons and works as a shepherd boy. He did not have the privilege of being either the oldest or the baby of the family, but he is his father's favourite son as the firstborn child of Jacob's preferred wife, Rachel. Jacob himself had had his life shaped by one parent, his mother, favouring one child above another, manipulating situations to make Jacob's life better than that of his older brother Esau. Her manipulation had wide-ranging and damaging effects (see Genesis 27) but Jacob had obviously not learned from his mother's mistakes.

Joseph tells tales to his father about his brothers and what they do in the fields while they are supposed to be looking after the sheep (Genesis 37:2). The seeds of his brothers' intense hatred for Joseph begin with this incident, and Jacob does not help matters when he gives a special coat to Joseph as a sign of his favour and love (Genesis 37:3). He is treating Joseph as if he were the firstborn of the family, not the eleventh, and this special treatment creates even more envy and anger among the brothers. You get the distinct impression that Joseph was seen as the proverbial 'pain in the neck'. And while his father could well have been thinking of him as a dutiful and loving son, at the same time Joseph could be seen as playing on his father's affections and manipulating him to treat him as superior to his brothers.

At this stage of Joseph's life, he is a 17-year-old who is immature and selfish in his relationships with other people. It sounds as if he did not think before he spoke, as if he were headstrong, full of himself and impulsive. Then something very extraordinary happens: God speaks into his life through two dreams. The first dream pictures a field, with Joseph at work with his brothers, binding sheaves of corn. Joseph's sheaf stands up and the brothers' sheaves all gather round it, bowing low before it (Genesis 37:6–7). The second dream shows the sun, moon and eleven stars bowing down to Joseph (Genesis 37:9–10).

When Joseph hears from God in this way, he does what most of us would do: he goes to tell someone what he thinks God has said to him. But the Bible tells us that Joseph was proud and boastful when he reported the dreams to his brothers. If he had been wiser, less impulsive, he might have considered first what the result of his actions would be. You can just picture the scene—Joseph in his ornate coat, arrogantly describing how God had not only spoken to him, but promised him that he would one day be superior to the

whole family. The brothers probably stood around him, hating him, and thinking, 'We have had just about our fill of this boy. We will get our own back—just wait and see.' In fact, even his father rebuked Joseph for his outspokenness (Genesis 37:10). But even taking Joseph's boasting into account, the interpretation of the dreams is clear. Joseph is in some way destined for greatness.

In defence of Joseph's behaviour, he obviously believed that his dreams were sent by God. So why not share what he had heard? Maybe, for once, Joseph wanted to be the centre of everyone's attention and feel important, not just the eleventh brother, albeit favoured by his father. Sometimes we might be tempted to take an impulsive course of action that in the short term boosts our self-esteem. We need to bear in mind that the long-term result might be adverse, that our actions might alienate people against us. Our judgment might be clouded by our own agenda just as Joseph's was clouded by his pride and arrogance.

Keeping our own counsel

At this point in the story, we can learn the following vital lesson—the importance of keeping our own counsel. If we feel we hear from God—through the Bible, certain circumstances, or a person—our first impulse may well be to tell someone else all about it. Our excitement may be such that all responsibility and sensitivity goes out of the window, especially if what God seems to be saying puts us in a good light! It is much harder to keep our own counsel, reflecting quietly on what we have heard. Our special insight may not be for sharing with others immediately or even at all—especially if we are not sure that we have fully under-stood it, or appreciated the effect it may have on our own or other people's lives. Like Mary, the mother of Jesus, we need to 'treasure up and ponder' these things in our hearts

(Luke 2:19). If Joseph had kept his dreams to himself, perhaps his brothers would not have plotted to kill him, and maybe God would have fulfilled his promises to Joseph in a very different way.

Above all, we should not tell someone else that they are involved in that promise from God, unless we are very sure it is right to do so. When I first started going out with my husband, David, I got a sense early on that he was the man I was to marry. Instead of keeping it to myself and pondering over it, just three months into our relationship I asked him to marry me. David's reaction was to act as if he had not heard me. I had frightened the poor man! I should have waited and let God take control of the situation. I would like to be able to say that I learned from my mistake, but in the course of our four-year relationship I proposed twice more! Like Joseph, I am not very good at learning my lessons or waiting for God's timing.

Slavery

As the Bible story unfolds, Jacob sends Joseph to Shechem to find out how his brothers are getting on with their work (Genesis 37:13–14). In the light of Joseph's tale-telling before, it was shortsighted of Jacob to send him again. It would not improve brotherly relations, as they would assume he had been sent to spy on them once more. As it was, Jacob would not see Joseph again for 20 years. Genesis 37:18–20 tells what happened: 'But they saw him in the distance, and before he reached them, they plotted to kill him. "Here comes that dreamer!" they said to each other. "Come now, let's kill him and throw him into one of these cisterns and say that a ferocious animal devoured him. Then we'll see what comes of his dreams."'

Later in Genesis, we are given some indication how Joseph felt at that moment, because when the brothers go to Egypt during the famine, they recall his fear, saying, 'We saw his terror and anguish and heard his pleadings, but we wouldn't listen' (Genesis 42:21, LB). So much for his special promises. He had begged for his life but as far as he was concerned, he faced a slow and agonizing death by starvation. I wonder if, at this point, he began to realize that he was partly to blame for his predicament. Maybe he thought back to his earlier behaviour and started to understand how it had provoked his brothers.

Later some traders pass by and, as the brothers do not want the guilt of Joseph's death on their consciences, they sell him and plan to make his disappearance look as if a wild animal has killed him (Genesis 37:31). When Joseph was lifted out of the well, he must have felt relief: had his brothers decided to spare him? Maybe it had been some ghastly mistake or joke after all. But his relief was short-lived. He realized that he had been sold as a slave and was being taken to Egypt. This may have simply felt like a postponement of death—after all, slaves would not generally expect to live very long. This is what we could call Joseph's 'humbling' stage: in a matter of hours he goes from being the favoured son to becoming a slave, taken away from home, the place of blessing and covenant, to a foreign land.

As if riding on the downward spiral of a rollercoaster, Joseph was being plunged into disappointment in his walk with God. Until this point, he had travelled on an upward curve of rising expectation with nothing particularly bad happening to him. From now on, however, he would experience both highs and lows.

The rollercoaster of life

As Christians, we are ill-prepared for a rollercoaster experience of life. We are content for the 'highs' to happen, and maybe one low point, but not for the continuing difficulties that can characterize much of our Christian lives. We view events like miscarriages, cancer and losing a job as terrible surprises, as God failing us. Most of us—unconsciously or otherwise—expect that when we become Christians our lives will improve. We somehow assume that only good things happen to God's people. We often see the 'lows' as a sign of failure, rather than part of a steady progression towards the goal God has for each of our lives.

Like what happened to Joseph, we may find events taking us further away from our dream. We can be deflected from our trust in the promises of God by circumstances apparently out of our control. We feel panic set in when we realize that the 'high' we were experiencing has just turned into yet another low. And then, instead of holding on to what we feel God has said to us, we may decide that we misheard or misinterpreted him. We reject the promise altogether rather than persevering and waiting, and sometimes it may take an objective third party to remind us of what God is clearly doing in our life. We are often too emotionally involved in the situation to see clearly, and it is vital that we step back and take stock, however hard that may seem. A good example of this is someone who feels that they have been called to overseas mission work, but encounters repeated obstacles that prevent them from starting. A wise friend may help them to see that God is actually calling them to serve him right where they are for the moment and that maybe an avenue for wider work will open later.

Potiphar's house

When we meet Joseph again, he has been sold to Potiphar, who is captain of the king's bodyguard in Egypt and chief executioner (Genesis 39:1). This could be viewed as a positive move. Potiphar would have been a respected man and his slaves would probably have felt that they had 'landed on their feet' on arriving in his household. So this heralds the beginning of what we could call the 'stability stage' in Joseph's life. He seems to accept his situation and does his new job to the best of his ability, and it is not long before Potiphar recognizes that 'the Lord was with Joseph in a very special way' (Genesis 39:3, LB). Joseph rises to a position of trust, and Potiphar puts him in charge of all his household and business affairs. Although it was not surprising for slaves to rise to responsible positions in a household, Joseph was possibly unusual in that no Egyptian would normally put all his affairs in the hands of a foreigner.

According to the Bible account, Joseph spends ten years in Potiphar's household without any further dramatic events. Although he is still a slave, and has by now lived through most of his twenties, we can assume that he must have felt circumstances were as good as could be expected. He is in charge of a respected household and is highly valued by his master. Perhaps he hoped that sometime in the future he might even get back home. Maybe he even dared to hope that in some way, those long-ago dreams of authority might come true. But once again, life is about to take a downward spiral on Joseph's rollercoaster. Potiphar's wife throws herself at the Hebrew slave, making it quite clear that what she wants is him. It would have been normal if Joseph had given in to her. After all, he was just a slave, expected to obey without question. And the situation may have been more complicated: Potiphar's wife may have wanted to use Joseph in some way to get rid of her husband. Egyptian wives, especially those married to rich men, had been known to kill their husbands, and Joseph could have gone along with this, using the intrigue to better himself, hoping after all to fulfil God's promise.

Instead, he is brave enough to stand up to Potiphar's wife,

saying that if he gives in to her temptation, not only will he be slighting his master's trust in him, but sinning against God. She does not give up, however, and pursues Joseph until he literally has to run away from her, leaving his coat behind. No doubt enraged and humiliated, she cries rape and Joseph is thrown into prison. The fact that he is not given the death sentence (the punishment that the crime deserved) could suggest that there was some doubt in Potiphar's mind as to whether Joseph was guilty. Nevertheless, he chooses to go along with his wife's story and they both disappear from the narrative, leaving the once-favoured slave in prison.

This must have been an impossibly difficult time for Joseph. Stalked by his master's wife, he could have easily given in to temptation but chose not to do so. This could be a first glimpse for us of an older and more mature Joseph. After ten years of slavery, he had learnt to prize his self-esteem, dignity and godly principles; yet, as a result, he faced a false accusation followed by an indefinite prison sentence. Standing by his principles made his stable life plummet down a steep and apparently endless spiral of that rollercoaster of life.

Not guilty

While we may not actually find ourselves in prison 'at Her Majesty's pleasure', do we not often face comparable situations? Life seems good, we are happy and contented, and feel we are on the right road with God—and then the bubble bursts. The situation changes without any clear warning. Temptation can come along in many guises: it may be the opportunity of an affair, which we may or may not find ourselves able to resist. Equally we may want to ignore a dishonest practice at work but feel compelled to make a stand. We may be tempted to cheat financially but choose to send in an honest tax return. And when we do these things, making a godly stand, we may find to our shock and surprise that, instead of everything going right for us, as we would expect, our lives take a turn for the worse. This may be next to impossible for us to understand, especially as we feel we have 'done the right thing'. So what can we learn from how Joseph coped with his predicament?

Joseph now enters a 'disaster stage'. He is sent as an innocent man to what was quite possibly the worst prison in Egypt. People only went to Pharaoh's prison if they were accused of a serious crime such as treason, and once they were there, execution or death from natural causes were the only ways of getting out. But Joseph's disastrous situation improves slightly when the chief jailer puts him in charge of the prison administration. The Bible tells us that 'the Lord was with him so that everything ran smoothly and well' (Genesis 39:23, LB). In this way Joseph comes to meet the chief baker and the wine taster of the royal household. When he notices them looking worried one morning, they explain that they have both had dreams—and the very fact that worried faces were noteworthy in this terrible place is perhaps a sign that Joseph's good work had produced some improvements!

Joseph now reveals the depth of his trust in God by telling the baker and the wine taster that he might, with God's help, be able to explain their dreams. Although his own heaven-set dreams appeared to have come to nothing, he still trusted that God could speak through the dreams of others. The wine taster tells how he dreamt of a vine, with three branches on it that began to bud and blossom, producing a rich cluster of grapes that he squeezed into Pharaoh's cup (Genesis 40:9–11). Joseph interprets this dream to mean that the wine taster will be free in three days and will return to his old job. The chief baker then tells his dream: he saw three baskets on his head, with food for Pharaoh in the top basket, but birds flew down and ate all the food up (Genesis 40:16–17). Joseph has to give the baker the grim news that he will die in three days and his body will be eaten by the birds. Three days later, both dreams come true. As the wine taster prepares to leave prison, Joseph asks him to petition Pharaoh to release him too, as he is an innocent man. But in another sickening downward lurch of the rollercoaster, the wine taster returns to the palace and promptly forgets all about Joseph.

Yet again, Joseph faces extraordinarily hard circumstances. He saw the interpretation of those dreams come true, yet his own dreams of a decade before were still no closer to becoming reality. We can imagine him, in the weeks that followed, thinking whenever he heard voices at the prison gates, 'This is it! At last I'm going to be freed!' Yet as the weeks turned to months, he must slowly have realized that the wine taster had not mentioned him to Pharaoh, or even remembered him at all. His hopes and dreams were dashed once again and freedom did not come for another two years.

When disaster strikes

As I have hinted already, I can identify personally with the rollercoaster story of Joseph. I married David at the age of 26, after a turbulent four-year on-and-off relationship. Once married, life gradually settled into a comfortable routine. Five years on, we had just bought our first home, I was managing a Christian company and thought that things would just carry on getting better. Then disaster struck. In July 1994, having never had a day off sick in 43 years, my father fell ill. After a number of tests, it was discovered that he had cancer and he underwent an operation to remove a kidney. Everything seemed to go well and by October he had gone back to work part-time. In November he returned to hospital after feeling increasingly ill again and in December we were told he was dying. At the beginning of January 1995 he died in hospital, aged 57. I was devastated, feeling inconsolable. Later that same month, however, I found out I was pregnant and that lifted my spirit. I felt I was being given a replacement life in some way to make up for the loss of my dad. But in April, at my first ultrasound scan, they discovered that the baby had not grown and that it was in fact dead. I was brokenhearted, feeling as if death was following me around.

At this point my mother was diagnosed as needing chemotherapy for cancer. Three years before, she had been told she had cancer but had not needed any treatment as it was dormant. More than that, her type of cancer could have stayed dormant for years and not affected her at all. Despite the shock of the new diagnosis, the doctors were very optimistic as she had the most treatable type of this cancer, with a 90 per cent success rate. During the first treatment the tumours went down significantly.

At the end of May she telephoned me, giving me the news that her treatment had been stopped. My immediate reaction was relief that it had worked. But my mother was still speaking and it took a few seconds for me to realize that she was telling me she was dying. I could not believe it. I could not believe that we were going to have to endure the same terrible process of suffering, death and grief less than six months after my father had died. I went up to Glasgow to help care for her, as she wanted to spend her last days at home. Six weeks later she died, only 55 years old. I would not want my worst enemy to go through what my family and I had to endure—a year of sad news, rising hope and then despair. I sometimes wondered where God was in all that happened. Most of the time, where he was concerned, I felt

I heard only silence. Thinking about the story of Joseph, I felt that, like me, he must have spent time wondering if God really was in control of his life and if he really cared at all.

God's perfect timing

Even as he sat, seemingly forgotten in Pharaoh's prison, Joseph was about to see God's perfect timing come into operation. The 'elevation stage' of his life was drawing close. Unexpectedly, the wine taster's memory of Joseph is prompted when Pharaoh has dreams that not even his wise men can interpret (Genesis 41:9). He sees seven fat cows come out of the river and graze on the grass. Then seven skinny cows come out of the river, stand beside the fat cows and then eat them. Pharaoh also dreams about seven heads of grain on one stalk, with each grain well-formed and plump. He then sees another seven heads appear that are shrivelled, and these seven heads swallow up the plump grain.

The wine taster remembers Joseph and tells Pharaoh about his ability to interpret dreams, and at long last Joseph is summoned to the court. Using his God-given ability, he explains the dreams, and Pharaoh is so impressed with his insight that he puts him in charge of overseeing the foretold years of plenty and the following years of famine (Genesis 41:40). Joseph is transformed from prisoner to Pharaoh's right-hand man, as quickly as he had gone from Potiphar's slave to prisoner. It is as if someone starts as an office junior and is promoted to company director on their second day!

Joseph could fill his new position only because he had matured through his many trials and experiences. At the beginning of the story, he was an arrogant teenager who roused his brothers' hatred to the extent that they nearly killed him. But after slavery, temptation and imprisonment, he had turned back to God. We get some insight into how Joseph felt about his life by the names he gave his sons in

Genesis 41:51–52. His first son was named Manasseh, meaning 'made to forget', because God had restored to him what he had lost in his youth. His second son was named Ephraim, or 'fruitful', because God had made him fruitful both when he was a slave and when he entered the service of Pharaoh. Far from being bitter or angry with God for what had happened to him, Joseph clearly saw that God had stayed with him and blessed him even through the hard times.

I would like to be able to say that I viewed my own particularly difficult year as positively as Joseph did, but it was not until three years later that I could say my experiences had had a positive effect in my life. During that time I went through periods of great anger against God and certainly could not see how any of the events could be fulfilling part of God's plans or promises for my life. I even doubted whether he cared for me at all. Despite this, God was gracious to me, and, looking back, I know now that he was with me even through very difficult days. And like Joseph, I was eventually rescued out of the darkest time. Three weeks after my mother died, I found out that I was pregnant again. It was initially a period of great concern, as there were worries about the baby's development, but as the pregnancy progressed it became the light at the end of a long tunnel. It made me realize that without God, there is no life, and with God, death is not the end but just the beginning of eternal life. Despite everything, God proved trustworthy, even if my circumstances at times had indicated otherwise. In May 1996, I gave birth to Euan, a healthy baby boy.

Completion

We now enter the 'completion stage' of Joseph's life. He has brought Egypt through seven years of good harvests. He has been saving grain in the years of plenty as God advised through Pharaoh's dreams, and now the famine has started.

As the most important man in Egypt after Pharaoh, he has settled down to married life with his wife Asenath and their two sons.

One day during the famine, who should enter his chamber to ask for food but his own brothers. They have all come to Egypt apart from Benjamin, the youngest (Genesis 42:3–4). And as they approach Joseph, what do they do but bow down to him? They have no idea who Joseph is, but he recognizes them immediately and remembers the dreams of long ago. At last the dreams have come true, and in stranger circumstances than he could ever have imagined. The young shepherd boy has become a wealthy, important and princely man. Revealing his hard-won wisdom and maturity, Joseph does not admit his identity before testing his brothers to see if they too have changed. First he accuses them of being spies and throws them into jail. He then frees all of them except Simeon, and tells them that Simeon will be held hostage until they return with their youngest brother, as proof that they are not spies (Genesis 42:19–24).

The brothers eventually return with Benjamin and Joseph arranges to have a cup planted in his youngest brother's sack. Pretending to discover the loss, he threatens to enslave the man whose sack holds the cup. When it is found in Benjamin's sack, Judah steps forward and volunteers to become a slave in his brother's place because of the heart-break it will cause his father to lose his youngest son. Joseph then realizes that they really have changed. He cannot hide his identity any longer (Genesis 45:3) and explains all that has happened to him, showing that God had turned to good everything that had taken place.

Fulfilling the promises of God

It had taken approximately 22 years for Joseph to see the completion of God's plan in his life. There had been many years of waiting through good and bad times, yet ultimately Joseph saw it all as a positive experience. By the time his dreams came true, he was a completely different person— a man of patience, stature and dignity. It was the waiting, the rollercoaster experiences that he went through, which turned him into the person who could fulfil the promise of God.

We often see waiting as a punishment from God rather than something positive. Why does God not give us what we want straight away? Yet waiting and enduring difficult times can build character and give us patience. I can say with certainty that I am not the same person that I was before my parents' death. Looking back, I would say that 1995 was the worst year of my life—but through it all I learned amazing lessons about God and about myself. My relationship with God is now deeper. My faith has been strengthened by being tested in the most difficult of times. Yes, waiting can be hard; yes, it can test us to the point where we feel sure we cannot get through it. When we do come through this, however, we can experience God as more real, more trust-worthy. Then we can know with confidence that he is a God who holds to his word.

The Lord greatly blessed Joseph there in the home of his master, so that everything he did succeeded. Potiphar noticed this and realized that the Lord was with Joseph in a very special way.
GENESIS 39:2–3 (LB)

3

Moses: The Long Road Home

God heard their cries from heaven, and remembered his promise to Abraham, Isaac, and Jacob [to bring their descendants back into the land of Caanan].

EXODUS 2:23–24 (LB)

This is as much the story of the people of Israel and their waiting as it is the story of Moses. When we look at the dramatic rescue and ensuing journeys of the Israelites, we can learn unique lessons about the successes and mistakes of a whole group of people in the process of waiting, and how they respond to God as a result. We shall see how it took 40 days for God to get the people out of Egypt, but 40 years to get Egypt out of the people. We can see how, in the times of difficulty, they revert to their slave mentality and selective memory of how 'good' their life in Egypt was.

Moses, the leader of the people of Israel, did not make a very good start to his godly career—committing murder, then running away and hiding for 40 years in the desert. Despite this bad start, Moses went on to bring his people out of Egypt, experience the parting of the Red Sea and deliver the Ten Commandments. He carried the weight of a young nation on his shoulders but eventually realized that he would not enter the promised land because of both his and the people's unbelief and disobedience. He had to continue wandering with them in the desert and wait for another 40 years, not to see the promise fulfilled but to complete the punishment set by God.

Prince and murderer

Moses had a special mark on his life right from his birth. His mother kept her baby son a secret because the Pharaoh had ordered all newborn Hebrew boys to be drowned—an early form of 'ethnic cleansing'. After hiding Moses for three months, his mother puts him in a basket and sends him down the river under the watchful eye of his older sister. The Pharaoh's daughter finds him and adopts him, so that Moses grows up in the palace as an Egyptian prince—yet, interestingly, still views himself as a Hebrew: 'he went out to visit his fellow Hebrews' (Exodus 2:11, LB). Life starts to get more complicated when he kills an Egyptian for hitting a Hebrew man and then tries to cover up his crime. The next day he attempts to referee a dispute between two Hebrew men, only to discover that his secret is out. His life in danger, Moses at this point does what several characters in the Bible do in a crisis—he runs away (Exodus 2:15).

When we meet Moses again, he has lived in the desert for 40 years and is a married man with a wife, Zipporah, and a child named Gershom. Forty years is a long time to live out the consequences of a mistake made in younger days, and it is part of God's grace that he meets Moses at this point when he might well have felt a complete failure. The opposite to Joseph, Moses changed from Egyptian prince to shepherd, and may have wondered whether he had thrown away all chance of helping his captive people.

We can learn this from Moses: no matter what you have done in the past, God can use you if he thinks you are the best person for the job. While he was a prince, Moses must have realized that he was in a position to help his people in some way. But when he intervened to defend the Hebrew man, the result was failure. His was an emotional knee-jerk response to an event he did not like, when he should have waited for God's timing, asking God for wisdom as to how he could use his princely authority. No doubt Moses felt in deep despair when he first ran into the desert.

Voice in the desert

God delivers his promise to Moses through a burning bush. Exodus 3:7–10 tells us, 'Then the Lord told him, "I have seen the deep sorrows of my people in Egypt and have heard their pleas for freedom from their harsh taskmasters. I have come to deliver them… out of Egypt into a good land, a large land, a land 'flowing with milk and honey'… Yes, the wail of the people of Israel has risen to me in heaven, and I have seen the heavy tasks the Egyptians have oppressed them with. Now I am going to send you to Pharaoh, to demand that he let you lead my people out of Egypt"' (LB).

Moses had probably come to a point where, 40 years after his mistake, he assumed God would not or could not use him because, in his own eyes, he was not worthy. So now, instead of accepting the call, he makes up a number of excuses as to why he should not do what God has asked of him.

First of all, he says 'But I'm not the person for a job like that!' (Exodus 3:11, LB). Moses responds in the same way that many of us would: 'Good idea, God, but why me? Joe Bloggs down the road would be better at the job and more qualified to do it.'

When the 'Why me?' excuse fails, Moses desperately tries something else. He says, 'If I go to my people (notice the 'if', not 'when'), they will ask which God sent me!' Moses is in essence saying, 'Who are you anyway?' God then tells him what to say to the elders when he meets them— he kindly writes Moses' speech for him! (Exodus 3:13–22).

But Moses is still not happy, so he tries a different approach. Exodus 4:1 tells us that he said, 'They won't believe me. They won't do what *I* tell them to. They'll say,

"Jehovah never appeared to you!'" (LB). Moses is trying the tack of 'I am going to look stupid and no one will believe God spoke to me anyway.' God deals with this excuse by giving Moses supernatural powers, so that he will have something to show the elders when he speaks to them. He enables Moses to turn his rod into a snake and back again, and gives him the power to inflict leprosy on his own hand and then heal it.

Yet Moses continues to make excuses for not returning to Egypt. He gets ten out of ten for perseverance! His next evasive move is, 'I'm just not a good speaker... for I have a speech impediment' (Exodus 4:10, LB). To this, God replies, 'Who makes mouths? Isn't it I, the Lord? ... I will tell you what to say' (Exodus 4:11–12, LB).

Finally, we get to the real reason why Moses does not want to do the job that God is asking of him—he simply does not want to go back to Egypt. 'Lord, please! Send someone else' is his next plea. Although God then gets angry, he still tries to make the job easier for Moses by allowing his brother Aaron, who is 'a good speaker', to go with him (Exodus 4:13–14, LB).

This is an amazing encounter between Moses and God. Moses is either very brave or exceptionally desperate to talk to God the way he did. And if we look at the excuses Moses used, we find that we often use the same ones today. If the suggestion is made in our church that we should go out 'door to door' visiting, I always use the excuse, 'I can't speak very well and the people will not understand my Glaswegian accent'. The 'Why me?' excuse comes out again if someone is looking for people to join the crèche rota. Finally, if someone asks me to give my testimony, telling how I became a Christian, I use the 'no one will believe me' excuse. And we can find that God lets us come up with one or two reasons why we should not do something, before it becomes impossible to avoid the task to which he has called us.

Despite having previously committed murder, Moses is still the best person to carry out the job that God has in mind—leading the Israelites out of slavery into the promised land of Caanan. It is interesting to note that God does not make a special promise to Moses as an individual. While Abraham was promised a son, and given a wider promise that his descendants would fill the land as far as he could see, God appoints Moses leader, with all the ensuing responsibility but apparently without any special reward for him personally. We should take note that God may sometimes expect us to take on responsibilities in our own lives, in order that his promises for other people can be fulfilled.

Freedom from captivity

We resume the story of Moses at the point when God sends plagues on the Egyptians, and Moses has to play a waiting game with Pharaoh. God continually tells Moses that Pharaoh's heart will be hardened, and that he, God, will do more miracles demonstrating his power (see Exodus 7:3). Some of the time Pharaoh declares that he will let the Israelites go, only to change his mind when one of the plagues is prayed away by Moses. It is only when Pharaoh's firstborn son dies, on the night when the angel of death passes over every household, that he relents and finally lets the Israelites go. Causing plagues was common practice among magicians and for a while the Egyptians may have thought that Moses was simply playing tricks, but even they realized that the power of life and death was God's alone.

In delaying the exodus of the Israelite nation, God was using his power to shatter Pharaoh's pride and arrogance so that the Israelites would realize that it was Jehovah God alone who had freed them from slavery. The Israelites had waited many generations, through times of great hardship, for the day of their deliverance. And even when Moses came, they had to wait a bit longer. In fact their captivity initially became harder, as Pharaoh ordered them to gather their own straw to make bricks, although it had previously been provided for them.

The people may well have grown angry with Moses because Pharaoh was punishing them as a result of his interference at court. They probably also felt angry with God because they must have prayed so often for deliverance, yet here they were still waiting for it to happen. Sometimes we too grow impatient with God because we long for a short-term solution, not God's long-term answer. The Israelites discovered that they had to suffer more in the short term to gain long-term and lasting freedom.

The range of emotions the Israelites would have experienced could be compared to the feelings of people who have been unemployed for a long time. They desperately want life to improve but they are stuck in an increasingly despairing cycle of job-hunting. From my days of working with unemployed people, I recall that when they first attended a Job Club or similar set-up, many of them were suspicious and reluctant to get involved in case they were disappointed again. When they learnt to write a good application form and discovered the skills of doing a good interview, their expectations began to rise, but in some ways their lives seemed to be getting worse because they had to carry on the painful process of applying for jobs and going for interviews. With their new skills, though, it was often just a matter of time before they found the job they were seeking so desperately.

If the joy of getting a new job is special, how much more amazing must have been the feelings of the Israelites when they finally left Egypt. It must have been a truly exhilarating experience. Not only were they free from slavery but they experienced the power of God at work in their deliverance, when he parted the Red Sea, letting them cross and then sending the water crashing down on the Egyptian army. The people had cried out to God and at last their prayers for deliverance were answered. The waiting seemed to be over.

Short-term memory

As the Israelites set off for their new land, we might expect that they would continue to remember this rescue with great thankfulness; and not just at the special Passover festival, set up to commemorate their deliverance every year. Surely such amazing events would impact their lives and behaviour for a long time to come. But after just three days in the desert, they set up camp at Marah and find that they cannot drink the water because it is bitter. Do they remember how God has rescued them from Egypt and taken them across the Red Sea? It seems not—they turn against Moses, who has to plead to the Lord for help. God gives him a stick to throw into the water, which makes it sweet and drinkable.

What short memories the Israelites have! Yet are we any better? How many of us have waited a long time for God to do something in our lives? When we see God act, we are at first ecstatic and overjoyed. Within days, however, we can be moaning again. Why? Everyday life brings us down to earth with a bump and we forget about the good things that God has done for us. We can only see problems looming, with God seemingly silent. Sometimes the past seems rosier than the painful present we are experiencing .

The Israelites continue to complain. The next problem is not having enough to eat, and they even voice their wish to be back in Egypt (Exodus 16:3). God promises them food—meat in the evening and bread in the morning—but the food comes with a warning: they are only to collect enough for each day, except the day before the Sabbath, when they will find enough for two days. By setting these conditions, God was trying to teach them that he would provide for their daily needs and that their journey was part of a greater plan that was under his control. Despite this miraculous provision of food, however, the troubles grow worse when they move on and once again find no drinking water. Do the people remember how God had provided water before, and wait for him to do so again? No, they do not. They actually get so angry that Moses fears for his life, telling God that if he does not act quickly the people will stone their leader (Exodus 17:4).

When the Israelites found that patience did not produce the situation they wanted—an easy life with no hardship or worries—they had to find someone to blame and so got angry with Moses. So often we behave just the same. We may receive an answer from God after a long time of waiting, but we still look for someone to blame as soon as things get difficult. It is all too easy to fall into the trap of thinking that just because we learn to wait patiently, the end result will be a smooth and untroubled life.

The rules and regulations

When the people arrive at Mount Sinai, God speaks again to Moses, promising that if they obey him they will become his holy nation. When Moses reports this to the people, they all declare that they will do everything God asks of them (Exodus 19:8). Moses goes back up the mountain, where God gives him the Ten Commandments as well as legislation covering every area of life, from how to treat slaves and widows to what punishment should accompany certain crimes. Exodus 20:18 tells us, 'All the people saw the lightning and the smoke billowing from the mountain, and heard the thunder and the long, frightening trumpet blast;

and they stood at a distance, shaking with fear' (LB). They are rightly fearful of God because they see this manifestation of his power. Yet after all this, while God is giving Moses the Ten Commandments on tablets of stone (Exodus 24:12) as well as detailed instructions on building a tabernacle tent, things go badly wrong. Even though the people have just witnessed the awesome power of God, when Moses does not come down the mountain immediately, they go to Aaron and ask him to make them a new god to worship and to lead them. Amazingly, Aaron agrees to do this (Exodus 32:1–6).

It could be argued that the Israelites must surely be the most forgetful nation in history! They have experienced God's provision, God's power and God's law, by which they agreed to abide, yet here they are reverting to idol-worship simply because they cannot wait for Moses to return. And even though Aaron had experienced the glory of God, alongside Moses, he appears to be swept along with the emotion of the situation, because on seeing the joy of the people when the calf-idol is produced, he decides to build an altar to this new 'god' and have a feast day. This feast day quickly turns into an 'anything goes' party with Aaron presumably looking on.

We are not told why the people did not wait. Maybe they got bored or maybe they thought something had happened to Moses. So why didn't they fall back on the laws that God had just given them, rather than reverting to the idol-worship with which they would have been familiar in Egypt? Mob rule is a dangerous thing. Some of us may have experienced how powerful it can be at a football match when just a few disruptive people can start a riot. Aaron acts to make the people happy rather than in accordance with what is right. Being popular as a leader can be more appealing than being godly, and so Aaron decides to abandon his responsibility to guide the people in accordance with God's law.

This story shows that there are two ways in which we can wait, two attitudes of the heart—one positive and active in faith; one negative, frustrated, angry and disobedient. Waiting with a positive attitude builds patience, expectancy and maturity, but waiting with a negative attitude builds frustration, anger and eventually disobedience. Even as Christians, we tend not to place a high value on a positive attitude towards waiting because our society is geared towards instant gratification. Those who do not want to make any effort to wait can in consequence fail to reach a measure of personal maturity. Instead of learning to persevere through a situation, they opt for the easiest, most instant solution.

Some churches can react in the same way as the Israelites. They experience the blessings of God but do not seek his guidance on particular issues, whether it is moving to a larger building or choosing a leadership team or youth workers. Sometimes a vocal faction in a church decides what they want to happen and then pressurizes the leadership for a quick decision. For one reason or another, the leaders cannot or will not stand up to this pressure and are forced into making a decision when they should have waited for guidance from God. The result can be division or worse.

Moses, friend of God

When Moses returns to the camp and sees the golden calf, he throws the tablets of stone to the ground in anger (Exodus 32:19). The Lord sends a great plague on the people as a punishment and tells them that he will no longer travel with them because he cannot resist the temptation to punish them! Yet Moses meets with God again and says that he will not take another step unless the Lord goes with him. Because Moses had found favour with the Lord through his relationship and past obedience, God agrees to continue to guide him. Moses then asks God to show him his glory. God's reply is, 'There is a place near me where you may stand on a rock. When my glory passes by, I will put you in a cleft in the rock and cover you with my hand until I have passed by. Then I will remove my hand and you will see my back; but my face must not be seen' (Exodus 33:21–23).

This is an amazingly intimate moment. God allows Moses a glimpse of himself, while Moses experiences the hand of God laid protectingly over him. We see here something of the deep relationship between them. Moses continually debates with God and argues on behalf of the people, as a friend would. God draws Moses closer to himself by revealing his own anger and pain. In the busy lives that so many of us lead, we often talk to God, but how many of us take time to listen to him? A relationship can grow and deepen only if we learn to understand the other person. Our relationship with our loving heavenly Father is no different.

God gives Moses two replacement tablets of stone to take to the people, and Moses spends another 40 days up the mountain without eating or drinking, receiving further instructions from God (Exodus 34) and repairing the relationship with the Israelites. For the Israelites, there now follows a period of stability and unity. They are drawn together to build the tabernacle and the ark of the covenant, which holds the tablets of stone. In total they spend a year in the Sinai peninsula, receiving further laws and instructions from God (Exodus 35—40). Although this is a further long period of waiting, it may well have been a positive experience because they were all involved in shaping themselves as God's special nation. Waiting does not seem so hard if we are working with others towards a project given by God.

Complaining again

When the cloud moves from above the tabernacle, it is the sign to move on once more (Exodus 40:36). They have only been on the move for three days when the Israelites begin to complain of the hardship they are suffering, wanting to return home to Egypt. This time, Moses' reaction to all this complaining is to complain himself! He even arrives at the point of telling God to end his life (Numbers 11:4–15). Some church leaders despair at times over their congregations when everything they try ends in complaints and criticism. The outcome tends not to be as drastic as what happened to the Israelites: God responded to the people by giving them the meat they wanted—not just for a day or two but for a month. However, along with the quails that provided the meat, there came a plague that killed a large number of the people. The Israelites had become small-minded about their situation and wanted their selfish needs gratified immediately. But they paid a high price for their complaining.

Many people have had to wait for their 'promised land' in difficult circumstances which may be not of their own making. In the property boom of the 1980s, many stretched themselves financially to own a home. When the slump hit and mortgage rates continued to rise, people found not only that they were unable to afford to make the mortgage payments but their property was worth less than they had paid for it. Some people ended up with crippling debt and even on the streets without a home. Some couples ended up living back with their parents while others, less fortunate, had to rely on local councils who placed them in bed-and-breakfast accommodation. More than ten years later, some are only just beginning to recover from the experience. Like the Israelites, some complained bitterly about their plight, blaming God and anyone else for their circumstances, but others tried not to get bitter and trusted God until the situation became clearer, even though they did not fully understand why it was happening to them.

Unfortunately for Moses, there was dissatisfaction not only in the ranks but in the leadership too. Aaron and Miriam, his sister, complain to Moses about his wife being a foreigner. They also express the opinion that they hear from God as clearly as Moses does, and that he has no right to claim an exclusive relationship with God. God is so angry with their behaviour that he strikes Miriam with leprosy, a terrible punishment as it made her an instant outcast. Aaron pleads for forgiveness and, thanks to Moses' prayer, Miriam is cured of leprosy but is still banished from the camp for seven days, until she is seen to be clean again. This must have given her time to think about what she had done but also made the Israelites ponder her very public punishment for rebelling against Moses (Numbers 12).

Jealousy is a powerful and destructive emotion. Some of us may have been in a church where one leader is jealous of another. It causes division not only in the leadership but also among the members of the church who feel they have to take sides. The unity in the church and its effectiveness are destroyed. Good leadership is about recognizing not only our strengths but our weaknesses and choosing not to envy someone else who has a gifting that we do not share. We may wish to enjoy that gifting too, but when our wish turns to envy, it stops us being effective members of the church because our energies are absorbed by the envy.

Ten to two

When the people are within sight of the promised land, God instructs Moses to send spies into Canaan—one leader from each tribe, including Joshua and Caleb. Venturing into the land, they find it full of good things, a land flowing

with 'milk and honey'. But they are also daunted by the inhabitants of the land, who seem to them like giants. When they report back, they concentrate on the size of the people, not the good things in the land. It is only Caleb who speaks up and says, 'Let us go up at once and possess it, for we are well able to conquer it' (Numbers 13:30, LB). Hearing the mainly negative report, the people start weeping, saying that they should elect a leader to take them back to Egypt. Moses and Aaron try to persuade the people that the Lord will be with them, but this only angers them so much that they think of stoning both of their leaders. God again becomes angry with his people and tells Moses that this time he will not only disinherit them but will also destroy them with a plague. Again Moses pleads on the people's behalf and God relents from sending the plague. But he declares that they must wander in the desert for another 40 years as a punishment for their unbelief. All the spies who gave a fearful report of the promised land are struck down dead, and only Caleb and Joshua survive.

Most of the spies could not see beyond the problems before them because they had stopped focusing on the promise of God. God was asking them to think of themselves not as slaves but as his special and chosen people, with the strength that came with that knowledge. Ten of the spies were overtaken by fear, their emotions clouding their reason, and they lost faith in God. They had fought battles with God at their side, they had seen the miraculous ways in which he had provided them with food and water, and they had seen God punish disobedience. Yet their human fear overtook them, and they forgot their earlier experiences.

Consequences

Can you begin to imagine how Moses must have felt? He had come so close to leading his people into the promised land, only to see their unbelief destroy the dream. He must have felt anger, disappointment and personal sorrow that he would not see the promise fulfilled for which he had worked so hard. And even though the Israelites repented of their sinful attitude, they still had to endure the further 40 years of wandering, as did Moses. In the end, even he was not allowed into Caanan because of his impatience in the wilderness of Zin (Numbers 20). Like the Israelites, some of us have to learn that although God may forgive our sins, we cannot always undo the consequences of our sins. The extra-marital affair is one instance of being swept along by the emotion of the moment but paying the price in the long term—often with, at worst, a destroyed family or, at best, a long period of rebuilding trust.

We might expect the Israelites to go back into the wilderness and use the time of waiting and wandering constructively, teaching their children not to make the same mistakes as they have done. Some may well have done this and prepared the next generation for living in the promised land. Bitterness can so easily grow from disappointment, however, and for some of the Israelites this takes over. One of the chiefs, Korah, conspires with another 250 leaders to overthrow Moses (Numbers 16). Moses intercedes on their behalf, pleading with God not to wipe out all the men of Israel as he has threatened, and God decides to destroy only the families of Korah and two of his fellow conspirators. He sends an earthquake that swallows up their tents and all the people associated with them. Then 250 other leaders are destroyed by fire. Despite this terrible warning, a mob gathers against Moses and Aaron. The end result is that 14,700 people die of a plague sent by God as a punishment (Numbers 16:49).

Often, instead of supporting the leadership in a difficult time, a church may become argumentative, unconstructive

58

and sometimes downright rude. We need to remember that as the people of God we have to look at the greater good rather the short-term effects of a situation. We do not need to fear plagues from God, but bitterness can be almost as destructive in its consequences in the life of the church.

Last words

Our final encounter with Moses is when he gives his farewell speech, as the Israelites come to the end of their 40 years in the desert. Moses too has been wandering and waiting all those years. His speech takes the form of looking back and learning from the past, holding on to the promises of God for the present and formally handing over leadership to Joshua. God then leads him to the top of Mount Nebo, from where he can glimpse the promised land, and he dies at the age of 120 years (Deuteronomy 34:5–7).

Maybe more than anything else in the Old Testament, the exodus teaches us about God's character through his interaction with the Israelites and with Moses. God was trying to build a nation dedicated to his will and mission. The people had come from a background of abuse, slavery and idol-worship, but God wanted to turn them into a trusting, special people who worshipped him alone. When God revealed himself miraculously in freeing his people, they expected that he would always provide for them in such a way. What gradually became clear was that God had placed expectations on his nation. He was not an idol, to be picked up and discarded when it suited them. He was a jealous God, and if they chose to break his laws, they would have to face the consequences. He demanded commitment to an exclusive relationship. Yet this side of God was balanced by the fact that he provided for their needs, protected them from other tribes and gave them the freedom they so desperately wanted.

The story of the Israelites also shows the importance of learning from mistakes, something that the Israelites conspicuously failed to do. And while they were a nation being shaped by God for a special purpose, our churches should be equally open to his workings and able to learn from our mistakes. The people of Israel continually tested God's patience, and although they had seen his miracles, they kept failing to trust that he would look after them. In our churches we need to remind each other about the ways in which God has worked and looked after us, so that we have hope for the future. Like the Israelites, we have the ability to undermine the work of God or enhance and develop it.

We can also learn a lot from Moses, whether we ourselves are in leadership or not. Moses was initially reluctant to take on the job that God had for him. He then experienced the thrill of freeing his people, only to realize the cost that God's calling would have on his life. He also suffered the pain of waiting in the wilderness, but he had to lead by example. It would have been easy for him to give up leadership when he lost the hope of reaching the promised land, but he continued to lead the people for a further 40 years. And Moses developed an intimate relationship with God that helped him to see events in a different light. He viewed circumstances, whether good or bad, through this relationship. He debated, argued and discussed everything with God. In the same way we can grow into a living relationship with God that affects how we see and experience all aspects of life.

There has never been another prophet like Moses, for the Lord talked to him face to face.

DEUTERONOMY 34:10 (LB)

4

Mary, Mother of Jesus: Handmaid of God

But Mary treasured up all these things and pondered them in her heart.

LUKE 2:19

Mary the mother of Jesus tends to be considered an unsettling biblical character in some church circles. People feel she is awarded either too much or too little status for her position as a pivotal character in the life of Jesus. When we look at Mary as somebody who received a promise from God, and then had to wait for its fulfilment, she can teach us much, whatever the regard we may have for her otherwise. The unique promise given her—to bear the Son of God, the Messiah—was one that she saw fulfilled in part quite quickly. But she had to wait over 30 years to see the promise completed, from the arrival of Jesus to the coming of the Holy Spirit. She learned to live with the expectancy and the disappointment that result from prolonged waiting.

Angelic encounter

As the first chapter of Luke's Gospel tells, Mary meets the angel Gabriel, who greets her with the words 'Greetings, you who are highly favoured! The Lord is with you' (Luke 1:28). The angel then gives her an unbelievable promise: 'You will be with child and give birth to a son, and you are to give him the name Jesus. He will be great and called the

Son of the Most High. The Lord God will give him the throne of his father David, and he will reign over the house of Jacob for ever; his kingdom will never end' (Luke 1:31–33). By the power of the Holy Spirit a young virgin will be the means of God taking human form.

Most biblical experts agree that Mary was between 14 and 16 years old when this happened, the age when most Jewish girls entered their arranged marriages. She was due to marry the local carpenter, Joseph, and the Bible gives no hint that she was from anything other than an everyday hard-working village home. She may not even have been particularly attractive to look at! It is tempting to assume that because she was chosen to give birth to the Son of God, she must have been beautiful, in some way socially accomplished and surely from a well-to-do background. What is important about this young woman is that when she hears the incredible news that she is to bear the Son of God, she does not make excuses as to why she could not possibly do the job. She describes herself as 'the Lord's servant', willing to do his work (Luke 1:38)—and this is despite knowing the shame and danger that this calling would put on her life. In Jewish custom, engagement was so intrinsically linked to marriage that the fiancée was called a 'wife'. Any sexual relations with a third party during this time were considered adultery and under the law a woman could be stoned for such a crime. When we consider her obedience, it is tempting to make Mary into a spiritual giant, an unattainably saintly character, rather than an ordinary person who had developed the kind of faith that we should all display when God asks us to do something. While Mary's was an exceptional calling, God also has a plan and a calling for all of us, and he longs for our responses to be, 'Yes, Lord, according to your will.'

Promise reinforced

The angel had told Mary that her older relative Elizabeth was going to have a child, although she had previously been infertile. Understandably Mary rushes off to visit her, and this encounter helps to confirm the angel's message. We can assume that no one else knows that Mary is pregnant at this stage, but when Elizabeth first hears Mary's voice, her baby leaps inside her and she is filled with the Holy Spirit, exclaiming, 'Blessed are you among women, and blessed is the child you will bear! But why am I so favoured, that the mother of my Lord should come to me?' (Luke 1:42–43). Elizabeth's reaction must have been an indescribable comfort for Mary, who then sings a song of worship and thanksgiving to God (Luke 1:46–55), a song which reflects some of the Old Testament psalms and Hannah's song of praise in 1 Samuel 2.

It is always good when God reinforces a promise so quickly after delivering it, although of course it does not always happen this way. We may feel God directing us in a certain way and, like Mary, we want to follow his word. This word may then be confirmed through somebody or something else. Friends of ours felt called to go and work on the Isle of Man, and although the island gives only a limited amount of work permits each year, the husband received the second to last work permit for that year. After much prayer and planning, our friends took this as confirmation of God's calling.

Returning to the story, we are not told how Mary tells Joseph, her intended husband, that she is pregnant. But we are told his response: 'Because Joseph her husband was a righteous man and did not want to expose her to public disgrace, he had in mind to divorce her quietly' (Matthew 1:19). Joseph clearly gave careful thought to his decision to divorce. It would have meant public disgrace for both himself and for Mary, but less so than exposing her pregnancy and opening up the possibility of her being stoned for adultery. And it indicates that he did not initially believe her story of divine conception. Once he has decided on this course of action, however, an angel appears to him in a dream, confirming Mary's account as true and saying that the baby must be given the name Jesus. Mary must have been greatly relieved when Joseph told her about his angelic visitation. It must have been good to share the excitement of God's plan with someone else, and also the uncertainty about what the practical details would be. We can sometimes find ourselves in a position where we commit ourselves to work for God without realizing how it will affect our lives later on, what the long-term implications will be for our lives. If we knew how time-consuming the work would turn out to be, or how much heartache it might cause, we would probably be less willing to take the task on board. This is why God does not let us see too far ahead but promises us enough strength for each day.

Bethlehem journey

Just at this point, the Roman emperor calls for a census, a counting of the whole population, which meant that people had to return to their ancestral homes. In Joseph's case this was Bethlehem, because he was descended from King David. Mary went with him, although she was heavily pregnant. It is not clear whether she had to go with him as a condition of the census, or whether this was Joseph's way of protecting Mary from the local gossips, who would count up the months and come to their own conclusions.

In the words of Luke, 'While they were there, the time came for the baby to be born, and she gave birth to her first-born, a son. She wrapped him in cloths and placed him in a manger, because there was no room for them in the inn' (Luke 2:6–7). Mary, like most mothers, must have thought about the birth, and how and where it would happen. With the census, her plans were thrown into disarray. Here she was in a strange town with no place to give birth, as the lodging houses were all full. In hindsight we know that Jesus had to be born in Bethlehem to fulfil the prophecies about the Messiah, but did Mary? She may have thought that because she was giving birth to the Son of God, the situation would be somehow different, perhaps with angels making sure they had somewhere pleasant to stay! Nevertheless, her wait for the fulfilment of her promise to give birth to the Son of God was over, but the full consequences of being mother to the Messiah were not yet apparent. A song by Kenny Rogers called 'Mary, did you know?' includes lines that express the wonder of the event:

> *Mary, did you know,*
> *When you kiss your little baby,*
> *You've kissed the face of God?*

Most Jews believed that the Messiah would be someone like Moses, filled with the presence and power of God. Here was Mary with God in her arms. What a thought to come to terms with, to try to understand: when Mary cuddled, kissed and looked at her baby, she touched and looked at God.

Unexpected happenings

The miracle of Jesus' birth is followed by other strange events. An angel appears to some shepherds on the hills, outside the city, proclaiming what has happened. The shepherds arrive to visit the baby, and Mary 'ponders' all these things in her heart (Luke 2:19). She had probably begun to realize that from now on unusual occurrences would become commonplace. After all, she had given birth to the Son of God!

When God acts powerfully in our lives, it can at times be scary. Many of us like routine and predictability. We like to think that others, more spiritual than we are, will be called to be missionaries, run soup kitchens, help to organize the toddler group or be on the welcoming rota at church. We do not mind being Christians as long as we are not expected to change our comfortable lives too much or mix with people with whom we have nothing in common. We can cope with church on a Sunday and perhaps a midweek meeting because they fit neatly into our schedules, but anything else would be taking our Christianity a little too seriously. God, however, can challenge us to be different and to live lives of flexibility, prepared for the unexpected.

As the story continues, we have two seemingly normal events in the life of a Jewish baby boy. After eight days, Mary and Joseph took the baby to be circumcised and formally named. The priest must have been a little perplexed at the name 'Jesus' because it was not a family name. Like Zechariah and Elizabeth, who named their son 'John,' this couple were giving their son the name that God had commanded, not a usual family name. And after the designated time for Mary's purification, 33 days after circumcision as laid down by the law of Moses, they went and made a sacrifice at the temple, consecrating Jesus as the firstborn male. The usual animal selected for sacrifice was a lamb. Mary and Joseph could only afford two doves, the alternative offering for the less well-off. And what should have been a routine event became something special.

At the temple they encounter a righteous elderly man called Simeon who was waiting for the Messiah. The Holy Spirit had revealed to him that he would not die before seeing the Lord. When he sees the baby Jesus, he takes him in his arms, saying, 'Sovereign Lord, as you have promised, you now dismiss your servant in peace. For my eyes have seen your salvation, which you have prepared in the sight of all people' (Luke 2:29–31). Simeon also speaks directly to Mary: 'This child is destined to cause the falling and rising of many in Israel, and to be a sign that will be spoken against, so that the thoughts of many hearts will be revealed. And a sword will pierce your own soul too' (Luke 2:34–35).

Jesus is just 40 days old when this incident takes place. Whenever a baby is born, the parents wonder how their child will grow up, and what he or she will become. Most of us just have to wait and see what happens. Mary and Joseph, however, are given an insight into the future life of Jesus. What would Mary have thought when she looked down at Jesus, a tiny, innocent baby, having just been told that he would cause her pain, 'like a sword piercing her soul'?

It is probably not until six months later, or more, that the family receive some distinguished visitors in the shape of the Magi, or wise men, who come to worship Jesus, leaving gifts of gold, incense and myrrh (Matthew 2:9–12). The first two were gifts for a king, but myrrh was the oil used to embalm dead bodies. In retrospect we understand the significance of these gifts, but Mary did not then know the end of the story. Imagine the scene: there is a knock at the door. Instead of a friend calling by for a visit, Mary confronts richly dressed strangers who enter and bow before the young Jesus and leave an extraordinary selection of gifts. It is yet another reminder (if she needed it) that he is no ordinary baby. And a further upheaval follows soon after: the family has to flee to Egypt to escape Herod, who is looking for Jesus in order to kill him (Matthew 2:13–15).

It is possible that, by this time, Mary's waiting was clouded by fear and great anxiety. She had the Son of God to bring up, for a mysterious and potentially dangerous destiny, and events seemed to be turning against them. The death threat from the king resulted in the family becoming refugees in a foreign country. It must have seemed as if God was calling her to a life of uncertainty, of unexpected twists and turns.

Many of us enjoy the lives we lead. We certainly do not want our days filled with the unexpected. But sometimes God wants us to give up our comfortable existence and be a little more adventurous, perhaps to risk losing all security and stability for his sake.

Hidden years

After the death of Herod, the family returns to Nazareth, where Jesus grows up (Luke 2:39–40). There is no further mention of him until he reaches the age of 12, when Mary and Joseph take him to Jerusalem for the Passover celebration. On the way home, Jesus goes missing and it is days later when his anxious parents find him back at the temple, talking with teachers who are themselves astounded at his understanding of the law. When Mary questions him about why he disappeared, his reply is, 'Why were you searching for me? Didn't you know I had to be in my Father's house?' (Luke 2:49). But his parents don't understand what he is saying.

In these noteworthy events Mary reacts primarily as an ordinary mother. Her son is nowhere to be found, and when she does track him down, she is amazed that he is talking as an equal with the teachers of the law. She is, however, also a little annoyed because of what she perceives as his lack of responsibility and concern for them as parents. Jesus' reaction is to remind them of who he is—the Son of God, who at that moment is in his true Father's house. This is the first time that Jesus himself is shown with an awareness of his divinity. It is hardly surprising that Mary and Joseph did not understand, but Luke 2:51 tells us, 'His mother treasured all these things in her heart.' She must have spent long years pondering the significance of the events of Jesus' birth and wondering what the final outcome would be.

Sometimes, while we are waiting for God to deliver a promise, and life proceeds as normal for a period of years, we may miss the moment when God acts to encourage us that the promise still stands. He may do this through a certain event or a certain person, reaffirming that he keeps his promises.

We do not hear anything further about Jesus until he is around 30 years old—the Jewish age of spiritual leadership. It is then that Mary begins to see what giving birth to the Son of God really means, not just to her but to a host of other people. The time of waiting for this moment may have taken so long that she almost forgot who Jesus really was. Was he not her eldest son, probably following his father's trade as a carpenter? But God's perfect timing was always at work.

Family difficulties

The next chronicled event where Mary and Jesus are mentioned is a wedding, where Mary involves her son in what is turning into an embarrassing situation for the hosts. The wine runs out, and after Mary asks Jesus to help, he turns water into wine, even though his first response is, 'Why do you involve me? My time has not yet come' (John 2:4). His mother clearly understood that her son had some kind of power to change the situation.

By the next time we meet Mary, Jesus has vast crowds following him and an established reputation for healing and teaching. But Mary seems to have grown worried about the impact that Jesus is having. She arrives to meet him, along with some of her other children, wanting to talk to him—even perhaps to bring him home. Jesus' reaction was prob-

ably not what she expected. Matthew 12:46–50 describes the scene: 'Someone told him, "Your mother and brothers are standing outside, wanting to speak to you." Jesus replied to him, "Who is my mother, and who are my brothers?" Pointing to his disciples, he said, "Here are my mother and my brothers. For whoever does the will of my Father in heaven is my brother and sister and mother."'

Here we have Jesus again asserting his wider calling and the mission of his life. It must have been initially hard for Mary to hear this. She seems to have felt a continual struggle between her instincts of motherhood and her natural inclination to protect Jesus, and the extraordinary, unprecedented role that she knew he was entering as Son of God. In the song 'Thorns in the straw', Graham Kendrick sums it up like this:

> *And as she watched him through the years*
> *Her joy was mingled with her tears*
> *And she would feel it all again*
> *The glory and the shame*
> *And when the miracles began*
> *She wondered who is this man?*
> *And where would it all end?*

Most of us struggle with the same thing from time to time. We are pulled between our everyday lives and our heavenly destiny. We may feel the pull of what God wants for us but daily existence can wear us down and deflect us from the right direction. We may feel that God has asked us to go to a particular country as missionaries or to do voluntary work of some kind. Then we get locked into a routine of jobs, large mortgages and having children, and suddenly we feel that we can no longer do what God asked because we now have 'responsibilities'. In some circumstances this may be the right conclusion, but sometimes it is simply that we are scared of what we see as the risks involved in following God's will.

The end or the beginning?

We do not encounter Mary again until we hear about her at the foot of Jesus' cross. We can assume that she would have seen the public flogging of her son and followed him as he carried his cross to Golgotha—the Place of the Skull. What must she have felt? Like many faithful Jews, she had been waiting for the arrival of the Messiah. As a young woman, she encountered an angel who told her that she would give birth to the Messiah, and here she was after 33 years, watching her son die like a petty criminal. Did the pain and anguish of her dying son remind her of old Simeon's words so long ago about a sword entering her heart? Her waiting for the unfolding of Jesus' life seemed to be over, but surely not in the way she expected. Maybe, however, there was some comfort for her in being given into the care of John, 'the disciple whom Jesus loved', as described in John 19:25–27.

The last readily identifiable mention of Mary is in Acts 1:14: 'They all joined together constantly in prayer, along with the women and Mary the mother of Jesus, and with his brothers.' They were waiting for the coming of the Holy Spirit as directed by Jesus before he ascended to heaven, and it would seem that both Mary and Jesus' brothers had taken the final step from being a sceptical, at times disapproving, family to being followers of Jesus. Mary would have moved on from simply being the mother of Jesus to accepting Jesus as her Saviour and Lord. And both she and the other disciples, as they met together, were waiting for what they were sure would be his imminent return.

We are not told anything else about Mary but it is quite possible that she did not lead a peaceful and tranquil life thereafter. When the Holy Spirit came, thousands of people became followers of Jesus and they would have needed discipling. The growth and change in the newly formed Church would have taken up the time and energies of all its members. As time passed, Mary would have experienced all the Church's highs and lows, persecution by the Roman authorities and from Jewish neighbours. And when Jesus did not return as quickly as the disciples had hoped, they all had to come to terms with that fact. Far from being over, Mary's waiting changed to waiting for Jesus' second coming, the waiting which all his followers since then have shared.

Many of us have, in one place or another, picked up on the idea that as Christians we deserve a comfortable and easy life. We like to skim over the trials and tribulations of the Bible, turning instead to the promises about 'living life to the full'! This also affects our attitude towards waiting. We want God to give us only good things and give them as quickly as possible. If we look at Mary's life, however, we see that God's way can be continuous waiting, for first one event, then another.

Mary can be an inspiration to us all: she was a women of great strength and character, no doubt shaped further by the difficulties she faced. Despite times of bewilderment, excitement, anger and pain, she remained faithful to her calling as mother to the Son of God, caring for him and loving him to the end of his earthly life. And after that, she joined with the new believers to share all their joys and sorrows, and the longest wait of all.

'I am the Lord's servant,' Mary answered. 'May it be to me as you have said.'

LUKE 1:38

5

Peter: Solid Rock

'And I tell you that you are Peter, and on this rock I will build my church, and the gates of Hades will not overcome it.'
MATTHEW 16:18

Peter is a popular Bible character because so many of us can identify with him, especially in the trials and struggles he went through to become the man God intended him to be. Peter was a man who was to fail Jesus in a number of ways, yet Jesus saw the potential in him and in the end gave him an incredible promise despite all his failings. Peter went on to become one of the pillars of the Church, a teacher and apostle, and in the end (although this is not recorded in the Bible) a martyr. Although he waited faithfully, he saw only a partial fulfilment of the promise Jesus gave in his lifetime, with the Church still under severe persecution at the time of his reputed death. For all his impatience and tactlessness, Peter became a man who did a great work for God, and this can be an encouragement to us in our own lives as Christians.

The fisherman

Simon, as Peter was first known, was a hard-working, practical, down-to-earth married man who worked as a fisherman. At some point in his life, he moved from Bethsaida to Capernaum with his immediate family and mother-in-law (to the place where Jesus visited them and healed her). It is at Simon's very first encounter with Jesus that his name is changed: '"You are Simon son of John. You will be called Cephas" (which, when translated, is Peter)' (John 1:42). Peter means 'rock': Jesus renamed him not for what he was—because, as we will discover, he was often impetuous, aggressive and judgmental—but for what he would become. Jesus saw past Peter's public character to his heart, and knew him to be a loyal and intuitive man who would come to recognize Jesus as the Messiah.

While today we do not encounter Jesus face to face as Peter did, we can learn to hear him speaking to us through prayer and reading the Bible, through other Christians and through the church. He may not rename us as he did Peter, but he does look for the potential in us, not for what he encounters at the beginning of our Christian life. This should give us all comfort, knowing that he looks past our mistakes and character failings.

We meet Simon Peter early on in Matthew's Gospel: 'As Jesus was walking besides the Sea of Galilee, he saw two brothers, Simon called Peter and his brother Andrew. They were casting a net into the lake, for they were fishermen. "Come, follow me," Jesus said, "and I will make you fishers of men." At once they left their nets and followed him' (Matthew 4:18–20). Here we have two diligent, hard-working men out fishing, making a living for themselves and their families. Jesus comes along and asks them to follow him, and they leave everything to do so. This happened at the beginning of Jesus' ministry, so we can assume that he had not yet established a major reputation as a teacher or healer. Nevertheless, Peter and Andrew leave their jobs and families to become disciples, travelling round with this man. In fact, many commentators think that the disciples would have lived away from their families for the three years that they were with Jesus.

Like us, Simon was just an ordinary person out to make a

living to support his family—hardly an obvious choice as a disciple, yet he goes on to have his own unique encounter with Jesus. The disciples have been sent out on the lake of Galilee in a boat while Jesus goes up the mountain to pray. Later the boat is still some distance from the shore when Jesus comes to meet them, walking on the water. The disciples think he is a ghost, but Jesus tells them not to be afraid and Peter ends up getting out of the boat to come to Jesus. While he looks at Jesus, he finds that he too can walk on water. When he starts paying attention to the wind and the danger, however, he starts to sink. Jesus reaches for him, saying, 'You of little faith, why did you doubt?' (Matthew 14:31).

Peter goes from extraordinary faith one minute to indescribable fear and doubts the next. Many of us can identify with these swings of emotion. Some days we can feel that we are invincible as Christians. On those days, if someone asked us to move a mountain by faith alone, our response might well be, 'No problem!' At other times, however, being a Christian is hard work, especially when nothing appears to go right. We wilt and feel miserable under the pressure of everything. Has God changed? No! It is just hard for us to be consistent in our faith, even if, like Peter, we know that Jesus is very close to us. We suddenly notice the wind and the waves, God seems out of reach, and we fear we are going to drown. In the story, Jesus reached out for Peter when he started to sink. And so we do not need to worry. Jesus is consistent and dependable, and what he did for Peter, he can do for us.

A moment of insight

Peter hears the teachings of Christ and witnesses his healing ministry. Perhaps as a result of that, he has a conversation that will influence his life for years to come, a conversation that reveals the depth of his spiritual intuition. Jesus asks his disciples, 'Who do people say the Son of Man is?' They answer that some think he is John the Baptist, others Elijah, and others think he is Jeremiah or one of the prophets. But Jesus wants to know what they themselves think. 'What about you?' he asks. 'Who do you say I am?' And it is Simon Peter who answers, 'You are the Christ, the Son of the living God' (Matthew 16:16). Through the power of God, Peter is given an amazing insight into the character of Jesus, and Jesus then promises him what would be an unimaginable future for a working fisherman: 'I tell you that you are Peter, and on this rock I will build my church and the gates of Hades will not overcome it. I will give you the keys of the kingdom of heaven; whatever you bind on earth will be bound in heaven, and whatever you loose on earth will be loosed in heaven' (Matthew 16:18–19).

What an astounding promise—that he would play a pivotal role in the Church and would be 'given the keys of heaven'! Did Peter understand this message? He was not a highly educated man and here was Jesus promising him something beyond his understanding.

In a further conversation that Peter has with Jesus, however, we have an inkling that perhaps he had begun to understand what had been promised him. Jesus is teaching that he is the 'bread of life', but that in order to follow him the disciples have to become part of his death. John's Gospel tells of their response to this message: 'On hearing it, many of his disciples said, "This is a hard teaching. Who can accept it?" … From this time many of his disciples turned back and no longer followed him. "You do not want to leave too, do you?" Jesus asked the Twelve. Simon Peter answered him, "Lord, to whom shall we go? You have the words of eternal life. We believe and know that you are the Holy One of God"' (John 6:60, 66–69). Peter's faith is once again revealed in this moment of understanding who Jesus is. He believes that he has found the answer for his own life, and with growing excitement he must have been eagerly awaiting the fulfilment of Jesus' promise. We shall see, however, that this certainty wavers in the face of the unexpected.

Peter had undergone an intense spiritual experience. He was so sure of his faith and could not imagine ever feeling any different. Many of us can identify with Peter, because we probably felt the same way when we first became Christians. We were so certain of ourselves and were going to evangelize the world for God. Nothing would stop us. Yet when our faith is challenged, like Peter we can sometimes find it easier to deny what we know is right than to stand up for what we believe.

Denial and reinstatement

When Jesus tells Peter that he will deny him three times, Peter's response is completely in character: 'Even if I have to die with you, I will never disown you' (Matthew 26:35). You can just imagine the big rugged fisherman saying this, and at the time he probably meant it in all sincerity. Peter had followed Jesus for three years, witnessing his teachings, miracles and lifestyle, and he truly believed that Jesus was the Messiah. He was willing to lay down his life for him. Yet after the last supper, when Jesus takes Peter, James and John to the Garden of Gethsemane to watch and pray with him, they fall asleep not once but three times. Then, in the ensuing crisis of Jesus' arrest, Peter instinctively or angrily draws a sword and severs the right ear of one of the servants in attendance on the authorities. Jesus rebukes Peter for his action and heals the ear. In a short space of time Peter has gone from claiming undying devotion for Jesus to falling asleep on the job and then reacting impulsively, committing a deed that could have put all their lives at risk.

Worse is to follow. He defends Jesus in the garden, albeit

wrongly, but then he denies any link with Jesus when questioned by a young girl. He goes on to deny knowing Jesus twice more, until he is reminded of the warning that Jesus had given him: 'Then Peter remembered the word Jesus had spoken: "Before the cock crows, you will disown me three times." And he went outside and wept bitterly' (Matthew 26:75).

Despite all Peter's bravado, when push came to shove he let down both Jesus and himself. He believed himself to be a committed, dedicated and loyal disciple, promising that even if everyone else disowned Jesus, he would not do so. A young girl, a few people round a fire and a relative of the injured servant asked if he had followed Jesus, and he lied. In Peter's defence, we can assume that he was most likely confused, disorientated and afraid because of Jesus' arrest. His life may also have been in danger if he had acknowledged Jesus. In those moments of fear, however, all the promises and warnings that Jesus had given were forgotten: Peter ran scared.

Many of us have done exactly the same thing. We consider ourselves to be 'good' Christians. But if we are challenged at work or at the school gate with, 'Well, you're a Christian, what do you think?' many of us are suddenly lost for words and mumble something at our shoes. We do not want to appear weird or unusual, so we keep quiet in order to blend in. In doing this we can feel, like Peter, that we have failed because we have not acknowledged that we do know Jesus and that he plays a central part in our lives. On our own level we too can deny Christ.

When we next come across the disciples, they are in hiding. Their faith in Jesus has all but disappeared. By this time, Peter may have feared that Jesus' promise to him had been no more than kind words said by his master to keep him interested. Then, on the third day after Jesus' death, the women go to the tomb but find it empty. When Peter hears the news, he immediately rushes off to see for himself. He finds the strips of grave clothes and cannot understand what has happened. It is not long before he finds out! The risen Jesus appears and calms their fears, confirming that the news is true: he has risen from the dead.

Thereafter, Jesus starts the process of reinstating Peter into his proper role as one of the key players in the future of the Church. He appears to the disciples as they are fishing and has breakfast with them. After this breakfast, Jesus asks Peter three times if he loves him. Each time Peter says 'yes', hurt that Jesus is repeating the question. It is as if Jesus asks this question three times to balance the three times that Peter betrayed him. Just as Peter denied Jesus with his mouth, so Jesus makes Peter speak out his love three times. And every time he makes the right response, his calling as a leader of the Church is reaffirmed—a calling that will eventually lead to martyrdom (John 21:18). After this encounter, Peter could again live in the strength of the promise that he had been given. And now he would have to wait to see how it would be fulfilled in the years after Jesus had gone from them.

As Jesus restored Peter, so God may take us through a similar process of rehabilitation when we have strayed. We should never think that God no longer has room for us in his plans, so long as we come back and ask for forgiveness and seek his way again.

Peter the preacher and miracle worker

Events now begin to pick up speed in Peter's life, bringing him encouragement that waiting for the promise of Jesus would bring rewards after all. Jesus had told his disciples to remain in Jerusalem to receive 'power from on high'. The feast of Pentecost is approaching, a feast celebrated by all Jews 50 days after the Passover, attracting crowds of people to the city from many different countries. On the day of the feast, the Holy Spirit descends 'like the blowing of a violent wind' on the house where the disciples are meeting and they begin to speak in different languages (Acts 2:2–4). After this, it is Peter who goes out to address the crowd outside the house, giving what turns out to be his first sermon. Thousands repent and are received by baptism into the newly formed Church. Quite a start to a preaching ministry!

After the events at Pentecost, Peter and John go to the temple to pray. A man who has been crippled from birth stops them and asks for money. As Acts tells it, 'Peter said, "Silver or gold I do not have, but what I have I give you. In the name of Jesus Christ of Nazareth, walk" … He jumped to his feet and began to walk' (Acts 3:6, 8). This miracle gave a lame man power to walk, and it gave Peter the chance to talk to the onlookers who had recognized the man and were amazed.

Another less happy result of this miracle is that Peter and John are arrested for the first time, as the religious leaders fear the implications of their message. When they are summoned to explain themselves, Peter uses the opportunity to preach once again about Christ, and although the leaders command them not to spread this new teaching further, Peter refuses. And as Acts tells us, the leaders 'could not decide how to punish them, because all the people were praising God for what had happened' (Acts 4:21). Peter continues to work miraculous healings and to preach about Jesus, and he is again thrown into prison. This second time, he is freed by an angel who comes to open the door in the night.

Our experience as Christians is probably far less dramatic than Peter's. Not many of us see 3000 people saved after we have given a talk, or angels setting us free from jail! But we can experience encouraging times when, for example, we get a chance to chat to a friend or neighbour about our beliefs. Or we may see long-awaited answers to prayer for ourselves or for others. These times can help our faith to grow, boosting our ability to trust God. We may feel as if the waiting and the watching and patience all seem to pay off— but we must not forget to give thanks to God when we see him at work in this way.

Faith stretched

Peter would need to remember those encouraging times, because events were unfolding that would stretch his faith and his belief in the promises he had received. Almost immediately he has discipline problems to deal with, as is almost inevitable at times of massive church growth. A couple called Ananias and Sapphira sell some of their property to help the believers but keep back part of the money raised for themselves. Peter has to confront the couple about their deception of the fellowship—and, more importantly, of God. This confrontation ends, sadly, in the death of both husband and wife.

Another problem caused by the rapid growth in numbers was that some poorer members of the church were being overlooked when food was distributed. The twelve disciples appoint seven men to take over the food distribution so that the twelve could concentrate on proclaiming the gospel. One of these seven men is Stephen, described as 'a man full of faith' who 'did great wonders and miraculous signs' (Acts 6:5, 8). It is this boldness and wisdom that prompts his enemies to bring him before the religious leaders on a charge of blasphemy. Although Stephen eloquently defends himself, the council condemns him to death by stoning.

This must have been a major blow for Peter and the young church. Until this point, the religious authorities had threatened and imprisoned the church leaders but eventually released them with a warning. After Stephen's death, a more widespread and organized persecution of Christians began, centred round a man called Saul. Opposition is one thing to cope with, but severe persecution and even death meant that joining the Christians was a hard choice indeed.

Peter was now leader of a church under systematic attack. Seeing his promise fulfilled had until then been dramatic and exciting; now it was truly dangerous. Although he believed he might eventually die a martyr's death, he probably hoped that the church would be going from strength to strength at the time, not scattered and in hiding.

It is easy for us to believe that God is with us in the good times but not the bad. Waiting is easy if everything is going well with our lives. It is much harder if everything seems a struggle, and we may be tempted to think that God has let us down. We fail to look back and see his encouragement in the past—encouragement that can help us through the present. I love sitting at the top of a mountain on a clear day and taking in the view, especially on family trips to New Zealand, my husband's home country. Often there are two ways to reach the top of the mountain—by cable car or by walking. Most of us would probably take the easy option! If the cable car breaks down, and everyone has to walk, you can spot the people who are used to vigorous exercise and those who struggle because they are unfit. If as Christians we only experience good times and encouraging moments, we will be ill-prepared and unfit to cope when the hard times come. Walking up the mountain may be harder, but in the longer term it is better for us, and we may appreciate the view from the top even more when we get there! And sometimes we in the West need to put our 'difficulties' in perspective. It is rare for us to endure much persecution for being Christians but in some countries people risk their lives by believing in Jesus.

Peter's continued struggles

When Saul is converted to Christianity—becoming Paul, the great evangelist and church-builder—the systematic persecution of the church stops for a time. 'Then the church throughout Judea, Galilee and Samaria enjoyed a time of peace. It was strengthened; and encouraged by the Holy Spirit, it grew in numbers, living in the fear of the Lord' (Acts 9:31). Peter must have breathed a sigh of relief! Everything seemed to be back on course as far as the growth of the church was concerned. Like many of us, however, Peter was to discover that just when he thought he knew exactly what God was doing in his life, he was asked to view things from a different angle. When this happens, we do not necessarily like what we see. Peter was to be challenged not by external forces, but by his own prejudices and what he accepted as his cultural norms. We know that God's plan had always been that all people, both Jews and non-Jews, would come to him through Jesus Christ. Until this time, only Jews and Gentile converts to Judaism (proselytes) had attracted the efforts of the early evangelists. To approach Gentiles directly was unthinkable, and Peter shared this narrow view. It would take a major intervention by God to convince Peter that the Gentiles were in fact part of his plan.

Cornelius, a Roman military commander living in Caesarea, has a vision in which an angel of God tells him to send for Peter. The next day, Peter is praying on the roof of a friend's house and falls into a trance. Acts recounts what happened: 'He saw heaven opened and something like a large sheet being let down to earth by its four corners. It contained all kinds of four-footed animals, as well as reptiles of the earth and birds of the air. Then a voice told him, "Get up, Peter. Kill and eat." "Surely not, Lord!" Peter replied. "I have never eaten anything impure or unclean." The voice spoke to him a second time, "Do not call anything impure that God has made clean." This happened three times, and immediately the sheet was taken back to heaven' (Acts 10:11–16). Then the servants of Cornelius arrive and invite Peter to his house. Before the dream, Peter would have refused to enter a Gentile home, but now he accepts the invitation.

In accordance with the Old Testament law, Jews would not eat with Gentiles: Jews believed that certain foods were unclean, and that they would be polluted if they touched those foods, let alone ate them. For Peter to consider eating with Gentiles meant having a complete disregard for everything he considered Jewish. It would also affect how other Jews viewed him—they would consider him unclean. God was not asking Peter to do something easy or simple. It meant laying down something of fundamental importance to him as a Jew, knowing that it would cause criticism and potential division within the church.

But Peter accepts what God has said to him, goes to Cornelius' house, and preaches to him, with the result that everyone in the household is converted. This was the first time that Gentiles had heard about Jesus directly, and it would have been obvious to Peter that God had sent his Holy Spirit to prepare the hearts of these Gentiles.

This was not the end of the matter, though. Paul's letter to the Galatians tells us that Paul had to take Peter to task over this very issue: in Antioch, Peter was mixing and eating quite freely with Gentiles unless Jewish visitors were present, in which case he would set himself apart again (Galatians 2:11–14).

Peter was being told off for double standards by Paul, a relatively recent convert—not a pleasant experience! He had bowed to peer pressure, and most of us can identify with him in his struggle. If we feel God challenging us to move forward in understanding some aspect of faith or

Christian living, especially if it is something that goes against our usual view of the world, it can be difficult to put into practice. It can be particularly hard when we are with those of our friends who believe the same thing as we did previously. We may not want to alienate them by differing from them, even if we know the change is a change for the better. Peter was having to think through his Jewish identity. For us, it may be an issue of personal finance or accepting people into our church who speak or dress differently from ourselves. Whatever it is, someone may have to say to us, 'You hypocrite' before we really work the issue out.

Peter's letters

From the letters attributed to Peter, we see how the apostle was preoccupied first with the suffering people underwent for being Christians and second with the question of when Jesus would return. The persecution of believers, together with trouble caused by false teachers, was making it difficult for them to wait for the return of Jesus in the right attitude of mind. Peter urged them to be patient and to persevere, despite the difficulties: 'Therefore, prepare your minds for action; be self-controlled; set your hope fully on the grace to be given you when Jesus Christ is revealed' (1 Peter 1:13). Although believers were not facing physical threat at that time, it was a period of great hostility against the church. To encourage his readers, Peter recounts to them all the blessings that they have received through their salvation: 'If you are insulted because of the name of Christ, you are blessed, for the Spirit of glory and of God rests on you' (1 Peter 4:14).

Peter's second letter addresses the issue of false teachers and their influence on the Christians who are becoming impatient because Jesus has not returned as quickly as they assumed he would. Peter strongly implies that, in some cases, it is just as well that Jesus has not come back, because the believers would not be ready: 'Therefore, dear friends, since you already know this, be on your guard so that you may not be carried away by the error of lawless men and fall from your secure position' (2 Peter 3:17). The believers may be special people in God's eyes but with this status comes a responsibility to live godly lives. Peter's letters deal with problems that, as Christians, we still face today. How do we deal with suffering and how do we wait in a godly way for Jesus' return? It is all too easy to become preoccupied with planning our futures, living our daily routines, forgetting to live in the knowledge that one day Jesus will come again. Like the readers of Peter's letters, we are simply warned to 'make every effort to be found spotless, blameless and at peace with him' (2 Peter 3:14).

Peter started his apostolic ministry as an ordinary working man with flaws and failings common to all of us. He said things he should not say and did things he should not do. He gave in to peer pressure and often acted on impulse, sometimes with unfortunate consequences. At times he got into such difficulties that there seemed no way out. But Jesus saw amazing potential in Peter and destined him to become a major figure in the foundation of the Church. By the end of his life, Peter was still waiting for Jesus' return, still waiting for the Church to grow strong. He saw the fulfilment of the promise made to him, yet not, perhaps, in the way he had expected. The story of his trials and struggles can inspire us in our faith journey today, and in our experiences as members of that same Church.

The Lord is not slow in keeping his promise, as some understand slowness. He is patient with you, not wanting anyone to perish, but everyone to come to repentance.

PETER 3:9

6

Waiting Churches

Blessed is the one who reads the words of this prophecy, and blessed are those who hear it and take to heart what is written in it, because the time is near.

REVELATION 1:3

We move now from individuals who lived with God's promises to looking at the promises given to the seven churches of Asia recorded in the book of Revelation. The letters are full of both warning and encouragement to the churches, showing how they are failing to wait for Jesus' return in the right attitude, and instructing them on how they should be behaving. For the congregations who must have thought that they were doing well and were proud of their achievements, these letters must have been humbling to hear. And the letters written to those churches still speak to us today. Like those early churches, we await the fulfilment of the ultimate promise of Revelation 21:1–4 of 'a new heaven and a new earth... no more crying or pain' and Jesus' second coming. We too can learn the lessons taught to those early churches, benefiting from the encouragement and the warnings.

Each of the letters follows a similar pattern, starting with a particular attribute of Christ, followed by some words of encouragement, and then a rebuke or warning. Each letter finishes with a promise, to be fulfilled if the churches overcome their failings. The churches are set realistic goals and encouraged to give up wrongdoing for something better. In return, they can hope for the fulfilment of that individual promise, but also the far greater promise of life eternal when Jesus returns.

Who wrote Revelation?

Many people think that the John who wrote Revelation was a disciple of Jesus and therefore probably the son of Zebedee. He lived in Asia, just like the Christians from the seven churches. One fact is undisputed, however—John was a prisoner on the island of Patmos in the Aegean Sea when he received the vision described in Revelation: 'I, John your brother and companion in the suffering and kingdom and patient endurance that are ours in Jesus, was on the island of Patmos because of the word of God and the testimony of Jesus' (Revelation 1:9). He had been banished by the emperor for being a Christian, possibly to work in the mines. This would probably have involved hard labour, beatings, few clothes, insufficient food and having to sleep on the floor in a dark prison.

Through an angel, John receives a vision of the risen Christ, and is directed to write about what he has seen to the seven churches in the Roman province of Asia. These churches were at Ephesus, Smyrna, Pergamum, Thyatira, Sardis, Philadephia and Laodicea, established Christian communities that had been around for 30 to 40 years. The cities to which they belonged were generally prosperous and influential, but part of the reason for John's letters was to prepare the churches for the increased persecution that would soon come from Rome. It was also to encourage them that this new difficulty should be seen in the light of God's final victory over evil.

The background to the growing persecution of the churches was the increase in worship of the emperor as divine, and the persecution of those who would not worship him. The Romans saw worship of the emperor as a common act that unified the empire and its diverse citizens, so to refuse to worship the emperor was seen as a political crime. No Christian would have been able to take part in emperor-worship because they could not claim anyone but Jesus as their Lord. If they stood by their beliefs, they were treated as traitors. With this background in mind, let us imagine that we are in the world of the early churches and see what lessons we can learn from their situations.

Ephesus—church of the lost passion

Ephesus was one of the central cities in the province of Asia, a wealthy and free city, which meant that it was self-governing and exempt from having Roman troops stationed there. But Ephesus was also a centre for pagan superstition, and the church was susceptible to fraudulent leaders claiming to be apostles and prophets.

In John's letter, the church at Ephesus is praised for its hard work and diligence. It is known for refusing to tolerate false teachers: 'I know that you cannot tolerate wicked men, that you have tested those who claim to be apostles but are not, and have found them false' (Revelation 2:2). So far, so good. In their zeal to root out evil, however, they have forgotten their first love and enthusiasm for the Lord and for each other. It may have been that in their eagerness to get rid of evil, they have become rigid in their views. By seeing evil in everything and only focusing on the negative, they have suffocated fellowship. In trying to do right and stop false teaching in the church, they have become focused on just one thing and they have lost the core of the community: 'Remember the height from which you have fallen! Repent and do the things you did at first. If you do not repent, I will come to you and remove your lampstand from its place' (Revelation 2:5). The church is told to

remember what they used to be like and to become like that again. If they do not heed the warning, God will 'pull the plug' on the church.

This would have been a startling warning for the church, because they considered themselves an established centre for Christianity, pure and holy. Here was a church that could smell a fraud a mile away, with a reputation for throwing people out rather than allowing the church to be polluted by evil. They were a 'one focus' church, which concentrated on the negative—evil—without balancing it with the positive—fellowship. Many of us can identify with such churches. What starts with good intentions can become institutionalized, and what's lost is fellowship. The relational aspect of the church disappears because the focus is so much in one direction. What also disappears is that feeling of joy that people have when they first become Christians, and are sharing with others in the community. The warning to the church and to us today is never to neglect our 'first love', because it is so easy to replace it with something else.

In balance to this warning is the fact that the individuals in the church are given an incredible promise if they over-come all the attacks against their faith—the right to eat from the tree of life in paradise.

Smyrna—church under pressure

Smyrna was known as 'the crown of Asia', fiercely loyal to Rome and the first city to erect a temple to the goddess Roma. It was a cultural city with a stadium for games, a public library, a theatre and an 'odeian' or music academy. There were also a great many Jewish people in the city who were both influential and hostile to the new church, as most new Christian converts came from Judaism.

The letter to this church is one of praise, all encour-agement and without any rebuke for the Christians, who tended to come from the lower classes and slave population. It acknowledges that the Smyrnan church is suffering under great persecution, not just from the Romans but from the members of the synagogue. 'I know the slander of those who say they are Jews and are not, but are a synagogue of Satan' (Revelation 2:9). For no reason, mobs would suddenly attack the homes of Christians, smashing and stealing what they could. The letter tells the believers that some of them would be put in prison, but only for a short time. 'Be faithful, even to the point of death, and I will give you the crown of life' (Revelation 2:10). One day they will receive a crown of joy and victory and are promised that nothing will separate them from the love of God. The 'second death' (eternal separation from God) will have no power over them (Revelation 2:11).

Here was a church under pressure from all sides, living with constant persecution that would grow even worse. Most of us have not personally experienced such a situation and can only imagine what it would be like. Along with the persecution, however, may come stories of amazing healing, people's lives being transformed and dramatic church growth. In some countries today, Christians have to consider giving up their lives for what they believe, but in return they may find that God's blessing comes in remarkable ways.

Pergamum—church of carnality

Pergamum was another centre of culture and had a library with over 200,000 parchment rolls in it. It was also known as a centre of religion, with altars to Zeus and Asclepius, a god of healing, as well as in honour of the emperor. People travelled long distances to the temples for relief of pain and illness.

The church at Pergamum is commended for staying true to Jesus' name, although they live in a city that is the centre of idolatry. 'I know where you live—where Satan has his throne' (Revelation 2:13). They are warned against some of the practices of their fellow citizens, especially those known as the Nicolaitans, who had a policy of compromise with the world, especially on moral issues. The Nicolaitans believed that because God's grace covered all sin, they could live any way they pleased without fear of God's condemnation. God's judgment is clear against those who are thus misleading and seducing the church: 'Repent therefore! Otherwise, I will soon come to you and will fight against them with the sword of my mouth' (Revelation 2:16). If the church members overcome these temptations, they are promised 'hidden manna' (2:17), imagery implying a storehouse. God will give them a rich blessing. They are also told they will be given 'a white stone with a new name written on it'. Some think that this refers to a custom whereby a person being tried for a crime received a white stone if they were found innocent and a black stone if proved guilty.

Many of us would be able to identify with the church at Pergamum. They were trying to live a righteous Christian life in a difficult situation. In doing this, they were commended, yet they still found it hard because everywhere they went, they were faced with an easier way to live—following the example of the people round about them who worshipped at the temples. They were also tempted to compromise by people in the church who included certain aspects of idol-worship and liberal views on morality in their personal beliefs.

Of course it is sometimes easier to compromise our beliefs than to stand up for them 24 hours a day. We often want to be accepted by the people round us, but as a result our faith can become weakened and we find it hard to decide which issues we should stand by and which we can let pass. It takes looking back to God, to the foundation of our faith, to see what is the best way for us to live.

Thyatira—culture-driven church

Thyatira was a commercial town with no particular religious significance. Its main business interest was the woollen trade, with most of the traders belonging to trade guilds. Refusing to join a guild meant giving up any chance of commercial activity. The Christians had problems in joining the guilds as members often had communal meals in the temples, which would begin and end with idol-sacrifice and often degenerate into drunken, immoral parties.

In John's letter, the church is commended for its love, works, faith and service. 'I know your deeds, your love and faith, your service and perseverance, and that you are now doing more than you did at first' (Revelation 2:19). However, they are accused of tolerating false prophets. Some of them are asking why they cannot join the guilds and do not want to give up their business interests for their beliefs. Some commentators suggest that the Jezebel mentioned (2:20), who was calling herself a prophetess, was probably not one woman but a 'spirit of compromise' in the form of certain people who had infiltrated the church and were preaching a lowering of Christian standards. The people with this 'spirit of Jezebel' love their business more than the church, finding that claims of commercial success speak more loudly than the claims of Christ. If they fail to repent, they will be subject to great suffering and ultimately death. Those who resist these teachings are promised authority over the nations (2:26) and the power and supremacy that go with it. And a personal blessing is given—'I will also give him the morning star' (2:28). Christ is the star, so they will be given all his grace and glory.

This church faced a problem that we all face today,

namely how far, if at all, Christians should compromise with the world in relation to their jobs and careers. The church in Thyatira had allowed an influence to seduce it to the point where people were altering Christianity to suit themselves. People who came into this church for the first time probably saw a fellowship full of life, energy and prosperity; yet this prosperity was due to some people compromising themselves with the guilds. The church was blinded to its real spiritual poverty because the society round about prided itself on obtaining wealth, and this lifestyle had invaded the church.

Do the Christians in Thyatira remind you of any you know? We live in an age of job insecurity, where people have to be seen to be working long hours and often have to spend time socializing with colleagues after work or their jobs may be at risk. Yet these are not the types of people rebuked in the Thyatira church. The challenge here is for people who seek wealth for its own sake and build their security on money rather than God. Their ideals can infiltrate the church to such a degree that some people feel that because they are Christian they have a right to wealth and prosperity, whatever the cost. The tension between faith and career is a real one, but here we are warned not to compromise because the wrong way can lead to spiritual death.

Sardis—church in spiritual slumber

Sardis had been a great city with unlimited wealth but it had gone to war against Persia and lost. It lost because the leaders had thought the city was impregnable and had not done anything to defend it. It was built on a steep, rocky mountain, and when the Persians tried to invade, the Persian king offered any soldier a rich reward if they could find a way up the rock to the city. One day, a Persian soldier saw a Sardisian soldier drop his helmet and climb down the rock face to collect it—this was the city's undoing. The Sardisian soldiers went to sleep that night as usual, secure in the knowledge that they could never be invaded. But the Persians climbed the mountain and took the city. The imagery in the letter to this church is linked to themes of sleeping, laziness and not being watchful, as a reminder of the failings of the city's past. When the Romans came along, they rebuilt the city and it became wealthy once again through the woollen trade.

According to the letter, the church in Sardis has a reputation in the city for being spiritually alive. The first thing that they are warned about, however, is being spiritually dead. The church has lost its vitality and power. Sardis is a degenerate city, and it contains a degenerate church: 'I know your deeds; you have a reputation of being alive, but you are dead' (Revelation 3:1). The church is not under persecution because it is not doing anything that merits active opposition. Failure to change their ways will result in judgment instead of blessing. And if they are still found to be 'dead' on the Lord's return, their names will be erased from his book of life (Revelation 3:5). There are still a faithful few, though, and they are given a threefold promise: they will be given white garments (white signified festivity) so that they can be guests at God's banquet; their names will never be wiped from the book of life; and Jesus Christ will confess their names before God and all his angels. They are told, in effect, that Jesus himself will present them to the Father on the day of judgment. What an honour that would be!

This church was sleepwalking through its spiritual life, thinking itself so secure in God that there was no need to stay watchful. Its greatest strength had become its major weakness. Sometimes we are not attacked at our weakest spot, but at the place of greatest strength, because we take that for granted. Some of us will know or have been part of churches that just go through the motions. These churches often think they have everything under control but really they are sleeping and not active. While they are often viewed by others as being 'nice' places, they never offend or stand up for anything. And churches can also be proud, taking for granted aspects of their church life such as the worship, the children's work or the preaching. What is your strength or your church's strength? Are you guarding it or taking it for granted?

Philadelphia—church of opportunity

Philadelphia was a young city, established as a centre of Greek culture and language for the cities round about. It was a grape-growing area because it was built on a volcanic plain, which gave it fertile soil but also the risk of earthquakes and aftershocks.

This is another of the churches which is given no word of rebuke, but only praise: 'I know that you have little strength, yet you have kept my word and have not denied my name' (Revelation 3:8). The letter sets before the church an open door of missionary opportunity. They are promised that those who persecute them will be made to come and kneel before them. For all the praise, they are also warned to hold on to what they have been given in case someone else comes along and overtakes them, and win the prize they have worked so hard to gain. If they are faithful, the believers are promised that, through the grace and power of God, their enemies will be made to acknowledge God's work in their lives. Also, because 'they have endured patiently' (3:10) through the peaceful times, Christ promises that they will be protected when the time of temptation and suffering comes.

This small church lived in the insecurity of an earthquake

zone, but they are promised that, in God's temple, pillars will be raised bearing their names (3:12). These will not be supporting pillars but monumental pillars, like those stately pillars erected in honour of Roman generals. Those earthly pillars were inscribed with the name of the person being honoured, where they came from and the great battles they had won. The believers are promised that their godly names will be inscribed on their pillars in the new Jerusalem. In effect, God is saying he will give them the strength, recognition and security that they currently have to live without.

This letter can especially encourage those of us who attend smaller churches and fellowships. We may feel weak and ineffectual for the task we face, but if we stay true to God, he may present us with an open door of opportunity. We can think we are too small, or the church down the road is better than us. As far as God is concerned, however, quality can be just as important as quantity!

Laodicea—church of arrogance

Laodicea was originally a fortress city but grew into a centre for banking, clothing manufacture and medicine. The city had a large Jewish population and seemed so wealthy that it had no need of God. The people were proud of being financially independent.

This church is given no words of encouragement but one of the sternest warnings: 'So, because you are lukewarm— neither hot nor cold—I am about to spit you out of my mouth' (Revelation 3:16). Jesus condemns their attitude of indifference, thinking of themselves as spiritually rich when they are actually poor. The letter even goes so far as to say that it would have been better if they had not become Christians, if they were only going to drift in a meaningless fashion. The church had shut Christ out, and the imagery used is that of Christ standing at the door knocking, waiting for them to repent. Anyone who hears the warning and pays heed is promised a seat on the throne of Jesus himself (3:21).

This church had taken on all the trappings of the world around them. They were proud, arrogant and wealthy, and probably thought they had it all. They thought they had everything, but in fact they were nothing. Although the letter contains the harshest of warnings, it also contains one of the most famous verses in the Bible: 'Here I am! I stand at the door and knock. If anyone hears my voice and opens the door, I will come in and eat with him, and he with me' (Revelation 3:20). But this word was for the Christians, not the unbelievers. God viewed the Christians with contempt because they did nothing, but the letter shows them the way to repent of their indifference and come back to God. The promise given to these believers is that those who endure similar trials to Christ's on earth will be given the same reward as him in glory. God will judge us only if we do nothing—if we ignore his invitation to be with him. The worst thing we can do is to become a Christian and then let it have no effect on the way we live.

Waiting in good heart

The letters to the churches were preparing them for a time of hardship and intense suffering. The book of Revelation does end on a positive note, however—the destruction of Satan and a vision of the future paradise of God. The letters should therefore be seen in the context of that goal to which the churches are called—to ready themselves for the revelation of the glory of God and the restoration of his creation.

If we look at these seven churches, we can learn about how to wait with the right attitude. We are called to remember the enthusiasm we had when we first became Christians. We should not conform to secular ways which may be easier to follow, or become tired and cynical. We are warned that suffering and persecution will come if we are following Christ, but we are told that he will give us the same strength that he had, to overcome them. The greatest warning we can take from these letters is about the spirit in which we should wait: we should not become apathetic, because God's judgment is swift. He wants us to be true to our calling, however long it takes. God's rewards for our patience are great—a new name, Christ-like authority over our enemies and, greatest of all, the gift of eternal life. And like those churches, we are called to wait patiently until that day of judgment and our reward arrive.

I saw the Holy City, the new Jerusalem, coming down out of heaven from God, prepared as a bride beautifully dressed for her husband.

REVELATION 21:2

7

God: Waiting For Us and With Us

He is patient with you, not wanting anyone to perish, but every-one to come to repentance.

2 PETER 3:9

We have looked at a number of people—and churches—in the Bible who had to wait on God, some for most of their earthly lives. It is easy to look at the world from a purely human perspective, though, and forget that it is not only people who have to wait for God's plans to unfold. God himself often has to wait for his followers to complete a task. He waits for unbelievers to repent and come to him. There are many characteristics of God portrayed in the Bible, and we often focus on his love, his power, his mercy. It is not so often that we consider his patience. If we examine some of the stories in which God waited for people to act or events to happen, this highlights the fact that God still waits for us and with us now. We should learn to be patient likewise and wait for others.

After the fall of Adam and Eve and the murder of Abel by his brother Cain, God looked down on the earth and saw how people had grown wicked. He saw that, in only ten generations since Adam, the creation he had made in his image was no longer 'good' but only inclined towards evil. 'The Lord was grieved that he had made man on the earth, and his heart was filled with pain' (Genesis 6:6). God decided to wipe out the earth, except for one man, Noah, who had found favour with him. God told Noah to build an ark, promising that he, his wife, his sons and their wives would all be saved, along with the animals that God instructed them to take as well. The story is so familiar that we forget that at this point God had to wait for Noah and his sons to build the ark!

We do not know exactly how long the job would have taken them, but even if they were experienced carpenters it would have been a considerable amount of time. Why did God not intervene to speed up the process? Perhaps he was giving all the other people a final opportunity to repent. Maybe God wanted to teach Noah patience, endurance and trust as he persevered with the building work despite the ridicule of his neighbours: he would need such characteristics when the flood finally came.

God may sometimes ask us to undertake a task or make a sacrifice that seems eccentric, especially to those around us. We may feel called to give up the career for which we have worked so hard, and become a full-time worker in Christian ministry, or to leave our comfortable home and work in challenging circumstances overseas. This calling may teach something about God to those looking on, but often we learn a lot as well, developing the godly character traits that we need for the next stage of life.

Turning to the story of Job, we see God standing back and letting events overtake one of his faithful servants. He had to wait for Job to show that his love for God was not based on wealth and a comfortable lifestyle, when all of that was stripped away, but on the fundamental assurance that God was truly faithful and trustworthy. Sometimes we can feel as if God has abandoned us. We may even lose the things that are most important to us—our house, our job, even a loved one. Often our immediate reaction is to blame

God for what has happened. As I told in an earlier chapter, when my parents died I reacted by blaming God, even to the point of seriously doubting my faith. It was only after many months of struggling that I realized that if I gave up being a Christian, I would have nothing left. I still did not understand why my parents had to die so young, but I realized that God had not abandoned me. He was waiting for me to come to the point in my grief where I could hear him. If he had spoken to me earlier, I would not have listened, because at that stage I simply wanted to find someone to blame.

Jonah's story is well known to many of us—how he rebelled against God's instruction to go to Nineveh and prophesy against the wickedness of the city. As the story unfolds, with the episodes of ship, storm and great fish, God has to wait for Jonah to repent of his pride and disobedience before he can take up the task of prophecy again.

God often has to wait for us to accept that he really does know best. Sometimes he may ask us to speak about him to someone whom we do not particularly like, so we metaphorically 'run away' by ignoring and avoiding them! It may take many 'coincidences'—meeting them in the supermarket, or at the school gate, before we admit that we have been in the wrong.

Between the end of the Old Testament and the events at the start of the Gospels, some 400 years pass. Was God inactive or asleep during this period? No, he was waiting to bring to fruition his plan of salvation for the world— sending his Son in human form to die for us. God had to wait for the right time and the right person to give birth to his son. He waited for Mary and chose her to give birth to the baby as the one he knew would best fulfil the role of mother to the Son of God.

And the New Testament itself is full of references to God waiting for us to respond to his love. Jesus gave us a great insight into this characteristic of God when he told the parable of the prodigal son.

Like the father in the parable who sees his son returning home and runs out to meet him, so God is with us. He waits for our return. Like many of us, the son expects that he will be greeted as a servant, not as a member of the family. We think that God could not possibly forgive us for what we have done and that we will somehow remain 'second-class Christians', not good enough to deserve God's forgiveness. We forget that God has been looking out for our coming so that he can throw a party for us, celebrating our homecoming!

Another major theme that runs through the New Testament is the fact that God is waiting for his kingdom to be finally revealed. For this to happen, we need to play our part in telling others about him. God has to wait for us to do our work, as we are his hands and feet on earth. With our help, he wants to give everyone the opportunity to hear about him.

Knowing that God too has to wait should give us encouragement in our waiting. We are living in fellowship with a supernatural God, a greater guiding presence who knows all about us—our past, our present and our future— and yet uses us to carry out his will. Our history has been shaped by such partnerships as God and Abraham, God and Moses, God and Peter. For some of us, too, waiting may result in our lives shaping significant events in future history.

Waiting on God means letting him develop our potential. We all need our lives continually shaped and matured by God so that he can use us fully, even though this can be painful sometimes. Waiting on God means developing personal discipline. Waiting often needs to be an act of will on our part, as for most of us it does not come naturally. We have to learn how to do it. We have to make ourselves step back from a situation and take stock, even if the situation is

a bad one. We tend to try to find quick solutions to problems so that we do not have to deal with them any more, when what we should do is to take time to see what God would have us do. It is also true that many of us are always trying to see what is round the corner, what is about to happen. As a result, we can easily miss what God wants to give us now. And then we may end up unprepared for the very thing for which we have been waiting.

Waiting is often a frustrating experience and can drain us emotionally if we do not rely on God. But God makes us wait for a reason, and often we do not look to see what that reason might be. The time of waiting may be his way of preparing us for an irreversible change in our lives. Maybe we are trying to change our job to a different part of the country. It will mean major upheaval, not just for us but for our family. Instead of selling our house immediately, it takes a few months. We get frustrated, but the wait may actually be a God-given opportunity for everyone to get used to the idea so that the move is not so traumatic after all. We want to know why things are taking so long, especially when we feel we are doing God's will in the first place. What it means, however, is that we sometimes need to listen more closely to God so that we get the full message about what he is doing, not just the bit we want to hear.

And when we finally see the end to our waiting, we can quickly forget what God was doing in that time of waiting and what we have learned. We get so excited, that all the good work that has been done is undone in the blink of an eye. It would be good for us if, like the Israelites, we had a 'Passover' type celebration to remind us of exactly what God had done for us! Of course in our churches we celebrate communion to remind us of Jesus' sacrifice for us and how it redeemed us; maybe we need personal celebrations to remind us of those times of waiting. Some people keep a spiritual journal or a folder with relevant scriptures to remind them of what God did to end their waiting and what they learned from it.

Looking back at the experiences of Bible characters, as we have done, is one of the best ways of reminding ourselves to look for what God is doing in our lives and to be grateful and give thanks, however hard the waiting. Like the Bible characters, our relationship with God can grow closer as a result, even if it takes us outside our comfort zones.

For through the Spirit, by faith, we wait for the hope of righteousness.

GALATIANS 5:5 (RSV)

Day by Day with God

Daily Bible reading notes

You may be interested to know that BRF publishes, in conjunction with Christina Press, a series of Bible reading notes written especially by women for women. Each issue of Day by day with God covers four months of daily Bible reading and reflection, with each day offering a Bible passage (key verses printed out), helpful comment and a prayer or thought for the day ahead.

The notes are edited by Mary Reid, and the team of contributors includes Beryl Adamsbaum, Diana Archer, Celia Bowring, Anne Coomes, Ann England, Rosemary Green, Margaret Killingray, Jennifer Rees Larcombe, Christine Leonard, Hilary McDowell, Bridget Plass, Elaine Pountney, Wendy Pritchard, Christina Rees, Alie Stibbe and Sandra Wheatley.

See page 112 for an order form.

Also from BRF

In the Palm of God's Hand
A diary of living against the odds
Wendy Bray

A day-by-day account of coming to terms with a diagnosis of advanced cancr and the trauma of treatment. Written in the form of a prayer diary, it πis a testimony of how personal faith can transform the hardest of times, and how God's love and mercy still break through, no matter how tough the situation.

'Sharing a diary like this is about more than baring your soul. It's like taking your clothes off in public in mid-January and asking passers-by to throw snowballs at you. Not something you would do unless you hoped an awful lot of good would come of it, But here I am, doing it (sharing the diary, that is—I'm too much of a coward to attempt the illustration!) So I must believe in the good. Whatever good might result is God's to reveal. I would hope that it will involve glory to him and comfort and encouragement to others, as well as providing the occasional laugh.'

£5.99   ISBN 1 84101 196 7

See page 112 for an order form.

REF	TITLE	PRICE	QTY	TOTAL
196 7	In the Palm of God's Hand	£5.99		

POSTAGE & PACKING CHARGES		Postage and packing:	
Order value	UK	Donation:	
£7.00 & under	£1.25		
£7.01–£30.00	£2.50	Total enclosed:	
Over £30.00	free		

❑ I would like to take out a year's subscription to
Day by Day with God.

❑ (UK) £11.55

❑ (Surface) £12.90

❑ (Air mail) £15.15

Name _____ Account No _____

Address _____

_____ Postcode _____

Telephone No _____ Email _____

Payment by: Cheque ❑ Mastercard ❑ Visa ❑
Postal Order ❑ Switch ❑

Credit card no. ❑❑❑❑ ❑❑❑❑ ❑❑❑❑ ❑❑❑❑
Expires ❑❑ ❑❑
Switch card no. ❑❑❑❑❑❑❑❑❑❑❑❑❑❑❑❑❑❑
Issue no. of Switch card ❑❑❑❑
Expires ❑❑ ❑❑

Signature _____ Date _____

All orders must be accompanied by the appropriate payment.
Please send your completed order form to:
BRF, First Floor, Elsfield Hall, 15–17 Elsfield Way, Oxford OX2 8EP
Tel. 01865 319700 / Fax. 01865 319701
Email: enquiries@brf.org.uk

**All BRF books and Bible reading notes
are available from your local Christian bookshop.**

BRF is a Registered Charity